W9-DBZ-007

ESPECIALLY FOR:

Michelle

FROM:

Virginia

DATE:

CHOOSE EXTRAORDINARY

180 FAITH-BUILDING DEVOTIONS FOR COURAGEOUS Girls

JOANNE SIMMONS

BARBOUR **kidz**

A Division of Barbour Publishing

© 2021 by Barbour Publishing, Inc.

ISBN 978-1-64352-803-8

Published by Barbour Publishing, Inc., 1810 Barbour Drive, Uhrichsville, Ohio 44683, www.barbourbooks.com

Our mission is to inspire the world with the life-changing message of the Bible.

Member of the
Evangelical Christian
Publishers Association

Printed in the United States of America.

000661 0321 SP

ORDINARY. . .OR EXTRAORDINARY?

Every day when you wake up, you can ask yourself, will today be ordinary or extraordinary? It doesn't mean you have to have amazing plans for the day. Even if you feel like nothing cool is going on in your life (and even if really hard or sad things are happening), you can make each day extraordinary by putting your focus on the best place it can be—on God! Ask Him to teach you more and more about Him as you read the Bible, pray, and worship Him throughout your day. Ask Him to help you build faith in Him that is huge and strong. Ask Him to show you the good things He wants you to do. As you pray this way every day, watch how God builds your faith and courage to do what He has planned for you, in both good times and bad. He wants you to have the best kind of life, the life He designed you for, following the plans He has made that are unique and meant especially for you! To choose extraordinary means to choose God and all that He wants for you!

ALL GOD'S GREATNESS

Praise the Lord! Praise God in His holy place!
Praise Him in the heavens of His power! Praise Him
for His great works! Praise Him for all His greatness!
Psalm 150:1–2

Are you a morning person who wakes up with lots of energy?
Or maybe it takes you awhile for your brain and body to
switch out of sleep mode into wake-up mode? Whatever the
case, one way to help get yourself running well in the morning is to choose extraordinary thoughts the moment you
wake up—thoughts that worship God for who He is and all He
has done. The book of Psalms is full of songs and prayers of
praise to read and memorize and remember each day. Pray
them back to God kind of like this. . .

🌸 🌸 🌸

Dear God, I praise You! You are holy and so awesome and
powerful! You created me and every good thing in this world.
Everything You do is great! There is nothing You can't do to help
me and guide me and give me courage in this new day. Thank
You for being so wonderful and loving me so well! Amen.

EXTRAORDINARY LIKE DEBORAH

Deborah, a woman who spoke for God, was judging Israel at that time. She would sit under the tree of Deborah between Ramah and Bethel in the hill country of Ephraim. And the people of Israel came to her to find out what was right or wrong.
JUDGES 4:4–5

The Bible contains stories of many women you can look up to for examples of faith and ways God worked through their lives. You'll find devotions about some of these women throughout this book. First let's talk about Deborah. She was the only woman to serve as a judge of the nation of Israel. That's pretty cool! God used her to free His people from the control of evil King Jabin of Canaan. She sent for a man named Barak and told him the instructions God had given to defeat King Jabin's army, which was led by a man named Sisera. Barak said to her, "I will go if you go with me. But if you do not go with me, I will not go." And Deborah replied, "For sure I will go with you. But the honor will not be yours as you go on your way. For the Lord will sell Sisera into the hands of a woman" (Judges 4:8–9).

Dear God, Deborah was an extraordinary leader to be the only female judge of the nation of Israel and willing to fight enemy armies. I know You can do great things through me and help me to be brave like Deborah too. Amen.

September 28   Rebecca

Ruth

RAISED TO LIFE

If then you have been raised with Christ,
keep looking for the good things of heaven.
COLOSSIANS 3:1

Have you been raised with Christ? *What does that mean?* you might wonder as you read this scripture. It means you are a Christian who believes in Jesus as your one and only Savior. It means you believe Jesus is God in human form, the Son whom Father God sent to live on earth and then die on the cross to take away your sin (the bad things you do that disobey God). Jesus did not stay dead but rose again. And when you believe in Him, it's like you have been raised from the death that sin causes and you have the gift of forever life in heaven with Jesus.

If you never have prayed a prayer of salvation, or if you simply want to tell God again that you believe, then pray something like this. . .

❀ ❀ ❀

Dear Jesus, I believe You are God, and You came to earth to
teach us. Then You died to take away our sins and show us how
much You love us. Then You rose again to life, and You make
me rise to forever life because I trust in You as my one and only
Savior. Thank You so much! Please help me to keep my mind
always thinking about You and about heaven. Amen.

THE VERY BEST HERO

*The one who says he belongs to Christ
should live the same kind of life Christ lived.*
1 JOHN 2:6

When you look up to someone, like a famous athlete or amazing astronaut or cool celebrity, you admire certain things about who that person is and what they do. Wanting to follow and be like them might help give you courage and a good goal for your life. But to have a truly extraordinary life means you choose to look up to God as your very best hero, above and beyond all others. God the Father sent His Son, Jesus Christ, to earth to be a human being just like all of us and to be our example for living the best, most extraordinary, most courageous kind of life. And how do we do that? By reading and studying God's Word to keep learning more and more about who God is and how Jesus lived.

Dear God, I want You to be my very best hero and Your Son, Jesus, to be my perfect example of how to live. Please help me to love learning and growing in You and Your ways. Amen.

SING!

Sing to the Lord a new song. Let all the earth sing
to the Lord. Sing to the Lord. Honor His name.
Make His saving power known from day to day.
PSALM 96:1–2

Singing your favorite worship songs in your mind or out loud as you wake up is another great way to choose extraordinary and boost your courage for each new day. It's important to fill your mind with the right kind of music. Many songs with lyrics that are not about God can be just for fun and totally okay to enjoy! Sadly, though, when some songs of this world repeat over and over in your brain, they can influence you more than you realize—and end up being really bad for you. So the best songs to focus on are those about God that remind you how awesome He is and how much He loves you and wants to help you.

Dear God, thank You for the gift of music in this world!
Please help me to love the music and songs that
make me think of You most of all. Amen.

THE MOST EXTRAORDINARY BOOK

God's Word is living and powerful.
HEBREWS 4:12

God's Word, the Bible, is the most extraordinary book of all time. It's not a book to read once and put back on the shelf; it's a constant, living guide for your life. God uses all of it to teach you and guide you in everything. Read what 2 Timothy 3:15–17 says: "You have known the Holy Writings since you were a child. They are able to give you wisdom that leads to being saved from the punishment of sin by putting your trust in Christ Jesus. All the Holy Writings are God-given and are made alive by Him. Man is helped when he is taught God's Word. It shows what is wrong. It changes the way of a man's life. It shows him how to be right with God. It gives the man who belongs to God everything he needs to work well for Him."

🌸 🌸 🌸

Dear God, I know Your Word isn't just for men but for all people, and that means I'm included. Help me to love and learn from Your extraordinary living Word and to be guided by it every single day. Amen.

EXTRAORDINARY MAKEOVER

Do not act like the sinful people of the world. Let God
change your life. First of all, let Him give you a new mind.
Then you will know what God wants you to do. And the
things you do will be good and pleasing and perfect.
ROMANS 12:2

God wants to give you an extraordinary makeover when you
trust in Jesus as your Savior and choose to follow Him. He
wants to change your life and your mind in the best kind of
way! Ask Him every day to help you not to act like the sinful people of this world. Ask Him to give you a mind like His,
to help you see things the way He does and do the things
He wants you to do. Ask Him to give you love, joy, peace,
patience, kindness, goodness, faithfulness, gentleness, and
self-control. Ask Him to help you grow in grace and truth and
to help you serve and care for others so that others will want
to know Him as Savior too!

Dear God, please give me the new life and
mind You want for me, a life and mind
that match up with Yours. Amen.

EXTRAORDINARY SHINE

"You are the light of the world. You cannot hide a city that is on a mountain. Men do not light a lamp and put it under a basket. They put it on a table so it gives light to all in the house. Let your light shine in front of men. Then they will see the good things you do and will honor your Father Who is in heaven."
MATTHEW 5:14–16

If you've trusted Jesus as your Savior, you have a beautiful shine to you because of God's Holy Spirit living in you. And you don't ever want to hide that shining light. Like this scripture says, you don't turn on a lamp and then hide it under a basket. That's silly. You should do good things with your life that bring honor to God and tell people why you do them—to praise and worship God and to share His love with others. Through your shine, let others see God's great love and His power to save people from sin.

Dear God, please help me keep on shining.
I don't ever want to hide my light! Amen.

ALL YOUR HEART, ALL FOR GOD

Whatever work you do, do it with all your heart. Do it for the Lord and not for men. Remember that you will get your reward from the Lord. He will give you what you should receive. You are working for the Lord Christ.
COLOSSIANS 3:23–24

You probably get told to "do your best" a lot, right? Like when you're doing schoolwork or chores, playing sports, or doing other activities. But maybe sometimes you wonder why you should. Maybe you feel tired and don't see why it matters whether you do a good job or not. Maybe it's hard for you to set good goals and meet them. In those times, remember this scripture from Colossians 3. Focus on working hard and doing your best to make God happy. Think of everything you do with the abilities He has given you as a way to honor and worship Him. That will motivate you like nothing else can, especially when you remember that God loves to watch and reward you in all kinds of ways, both here on earth and forever in heaven.

Dear God, remind me why I should work hard and do my best. It's because everything I do is for You! Pleasing You should be my motivation in everything. Sometimes doing my best just seems hard, so please help me. Amen.

EXTRAORDINARY LIKE A YOUNG SERVANT GIRL

*Naaman the captain of the army of the king of Syria was an
important man to his king. He was much respected. . .but he
had a bad skin disease. Now the Syrians had gone out in groups
of soldiers, and had taken a little girl from the land of Israel.
She served Naaman's wife. And she said to her owner, "I wish
that my owner's husband were with the man of God who is
in Samaria! Then he would heal his bad skin disease."*

2 Kings 5:1–3

You would think a respected and important army captain
might not listen to a simple young servant girl from Israel,
but Naaman did. Because of what she said, he was willing to
go to the man Elisha who was a prophet of our one true God
to see if his bad skin disease could be healed. If you read the
whole story, you will find that Naaman was healed and then
he believed in God alone! The servant girl was brave to speak
up and share her faith in God. She trusted that He had the
power to heal through His prophet Elisha.

*Dear God, help me to be brave like the servant girl
who spoke up to share her faith with Naaman. Thank
You for healing Naaman and showing Your power and
bringing more people to great faith in You! Amen.*

DEEP ROOTS

*As you have put your trust in Christ Jesus the Lord
to save you from the punishment of sin, now let Him
lead you in every step. Have your roots planted deep
in Christ. Grow in Him. Get your strength from Him.
Let Him make you strong in the faith as you have been
taught. Your life should be full of thanks to Him.*
COLOSSIANS 2:6-7

The deeper a plant's roots go, the stronger it is. And the
deeper you grow roots into Jesus, the stronger you are too!
Learn from Jesus and follow His ways, and thank God every
day for His many blessings.

*Dear God, please help my roots grow so deeply into
You that my faith becomes extraordinarily strong. Amen.*

EXTRAORDINARY PATIENCE

Give your way over to the Lord. Trust in Him also.
And He will do it. He will make your being right and
good show as the light, and your wise actions as the
noon day. Rest in the Lord and be willing to wait for Him.
PSALM 37:5–7

Have you ever watched a toddler throw a total fit because they couldn't wait for even just a minute to get what they wanted? No matter how old we get, sometimes we all feel like throwing a fit like that when we're waiting. Having patience can be really hard. We need God's kind of patience, and we need to ask Him to give it to us. Ask Him to help you want His timing and schedule more than your own. And ask Him what good things He'd like you to do during wait times.

Dear God, I sure don't always have good patience, so please
help me to know how to wait well. Help me to want things to
happen in Your perfect timing instead of my own. Amen.

GOD'S GREAT VOICE

The voice of the Lord is upon the waters. The God of shining-greatness thunders. The Lord is over many waters. The voice of the Lord is powerful. The voice of the Lord is great. The voice of the Lord breaks the cedars. . . . The voice of the Lord sends out lightning. The voice of the Lord shakes the desert.
PSALM 29:3–5, 7–8

Think of the loudest voice you've ever heard. Maybe it's yours when you're cheering on your favorite team! But the loudest voice in all the world can never have power like God's does. Let this scripture from Psalm 29 encourage you. Read it, remember it, and trust in it—and let it grow your faith in our extraordinary God. With just His voice He can say or do anything at all! No matter what is going on in the world, God is always in control, always able to use His voice to help and rescue in the good ways He chooses.

🌸 🌸 🌸

Dear God, remind me of the power of Your incredible voice that is able to do anything at all! Amen.

GOD LIVES IN YOU

*We have seen and are able to say that the Father sent
His Son to save the world from the punishment of sin.
The person who tells of Him in front of men and says that
Jesus is the Son of God, God is living in that one and that
one is living by the help of God. We have come to know
and believe the love God has for us. God is love. If you live
in love, you live by the help of God and God lives in you.*
1 JOHN 4:14–16

What are you feeling scared of or worried about today? There
are so many hard and sad and scary things in this world, but
thankfully, you are never left to face any of them alone! When
you believe that Jesus is the one true Savior and the Son of
God, then God is living in you through His Holy Spirit, and you
are living with His constant love and help. So cool!

✿ ✿ ✿

*Dear God, I believe in Jesus as my Savior, and so I
need to remember that You are with me always to help
with any hard thing. Sometimes I forget, and I'm sorry.
Please fill me up with awesome courage as I come to
trust that You live in me and never leave me. Amen.*

EXTRAORDINARY ENCOURAGEMENT

*Let us hold on to the hope we say we have and not
be changed. We can trust God that He will do what
He promised. Let us help each other to love others and
to do good. Let us not stay away from church meetings.
Some people are doing this all the time. Comfort each
other as you see the day of His return coming near.*
HEBREWS 10:23–25

The Bible talks a lot about encouragement—we need it from
God and from other Christians, and we need to share it with
others too. Do you see the word *courage* within the word *encouragement*? Not only does encouragement help you feel
better when you're sad or stressed or scared, but it also helps
you to be brave because it reminds you that you have people
in your life supporting you and the God of the whole universe
loving you and taking care of you. So surround yourself with
people who encourage you in God's love and in His ways, and
make sure you're always spreading good encouragement too!

*Dear God, please give me plenty of encouragement
in my life. And please help me to pass it on
to everyone who needs it. Amen.*

NO ONE ELSE LIKE GOD

There is no one like You among the gods, O Lord. And there are no works like Yours. All the nations You have made will come and worship before You, O Lord. And they will bring honor to Your name. For You are great and do great things. You alone are God. Teach me Your way, O Lord. I will walk in Your truth. May my heart fear Your name. O Lord my God, I will give thanks to You with all my heart. I will bring honor to Your name forever. For Your loving-kindness toward me is great.

<small>PSALM 86:8–13</small>

Read this psalm and then read it again as a prayer of praise to God from your own heart and mind. Sing it to your own tune if you want. It is a psalm describing how extraordinary and unique God is. No one else is like Him, and He deserves every bit of your respect and your attention and your praise!

Dear God, You are so awesome and so good to me. Only You are the one true God, and I am so thankful to know You and be loved by You! I love You too, and I want to follow and worship You forever. Amen.

GOD'S PLANS

The Lord brings the plans of nations to nothing. He wrecks
the plans of the people. The plans of the Lord stand
forever. The plans of His heart stand through the future
of all people. Happy is the nation whose God is the Lord.
Happy are the people He has chosen for His own.
PSALM 33:10–12

Are you ever scared that someone might have bad plans to embarrass you or bully you or hurt you in some way? Hopefully not, but if you ever do, then remember this scripture from Psalm 33. God wrecks the plans of people if He wants to. He can wreck any bad plan that someone might have against you. And if He does allow something bad to happen to you, He has plans to make you stronger because of it and turn it into something good instead. Romans 8:28 promises, "God makes all things work together for the good of those who love Him and are chosen to be a part of His plan."

Dear God, I believe You can wreck any bad plan or turn it into
good in some extraordinary way that only You can bring about.
Your plans are always the best, and I trust You! Amen.

A HUNGRY WIDOW

Then the word of the Lord came to him, saying,
"Get up and go to Zarephath. . . . I have told a
woman there, whose husband has died, to feed
you." So Elijah got up and went to Zarephath.
1 KINGS 17:8–10

When the prophet Elijah found the woman, just like God told him to, she said, "I have no bread. I only have enough flour in the jar to fill a hand, and a little oil in the jar." She was sure that she was about to make her very last tiny meal for her and her son and that they would soon starve to death. But "Elijah said to her, 'Have no fear. . . . Make me a little loaf of bread from it first, and bring it out to me. Then you may make one for yourself and for your son. For the Lord God of Israel says, "The jar of flour will not be used up. And the jar of oil will not be empty, until the day the Lord sends rain upon the earth." ' So she went and did what Elijah said. And she and he and those of her house ate for many days. The jar of flour was not used up, and the jar of oil did not become empty. It happened as was spoken by the word of the Lord through Elijah" (1 Kings 17:12–16).

✿ ✿ ✿

Dear God, even when things seem hopeless,
remind me that You have the power to
provide in extraordinary ways. Amen.

HOLY, HOLY, HOLY

I saw the Lord sitting on a throne, high and honored. His long clothing spread out and filled the house of God. Seraphim stood above Him, each having six wings. With two he covered his face, and with two he covered his feet, and with two he flew. One called out to another and said, "Holy, holy, holy, is the Lord of All. The whole earth is full of His shining-greatness."

ISAIAH 6:1–3

In this scripture the prophet Isaiah is describing a vision he had of God, sitting on His throne with angels called seraphim surrounding Him and worshipping Him. Do you know what it means to call God holy? It means to lift Him high above all others, calling Him perfect and worthy of total devotion— meaning all your attention. Whatever is going on in your life, take time each day to stop and think about God's holiness and praise Him for it. He is above all and totally perfect and awesome, and He loves you and cares about every detail of your life. That is an extraordinary blessing to be grateful for!

Dear God, You are holy, holy, holy! I'm amazed by You and grateful for You! Amen.

EXTRAORDINARY LIKE RUTH

*They cried again in loud voices. Orpah kissed her
mother-in-law. But Ruth held on to her. Naomi said,
"See, your sister-in-law has returned to her people and
her gods. Return after your sister-in-law." But Ruth said,
"Do not beg me to leave you or turn away from following
you. I will go where you go. I will live where you live. Your
people will be my people. And your God will be my God."*
RUTH 1:14–16

The story of Ruth in the Bible shows extraordinary loyalty.
She and her mother-in-law, Naomi, and sister-in-law, Orpah,
all lost their husbands, and it was dangerous in Bible times
for a woman not to have a man to take care of her. So Naomi
urged the younger women to leave her and go back to their
homeland and their people there. But Ruth demonstrated
extraordinary loyalty to her mother-in-law, deciding to stay
with her no matter what. If you read the whole story in the
book of Ruth in the Bible, you'll see how God blessed Ruth far
more than she ever thought possible because of her amazing
loyalty and love.

*Dear God, show me whom You want me to show
extraordinary loyalty and love to, just like You did
Ruth and blessed her incredibly for it. Amen.*

POWER OVER ALL THINGS FOREVER

*After you have suffered for awhile, God Himself will
make you perfect. He will keep you in the right way.
He will give you strength. He is the God of all loving-favor
and has called you through Christ Jesus to share His
shining-greatness forever. God has power over all things forever.*
1 PETER 5:10–11

You know there are all kinds of hurts in this world, little ones
like stubbing your toe and big ones like losing a loved one. But
God's Word promises that all kinds of suffering and pain are
just for a little while in this world as we wait for perfection in
heaven. Meanwhile, God will keep you on the right path and
give you strength to deal with the hard and hurtful things of
this life. None of them can ever overpower you because you
trust that He has power over all of them.

*Dear God, I hate the hurtful things of this world, but I love
that You have complete power over all of them. I trust that
You are working to make all things perfect and pain-free
forever in heaven, for me and all who trust in Jesus. Amen.*

ALWAYS THE SAME

*You made the earth in the beginning. You made the
heavens with Your hands. They will be destroyed but You will
always live. They will all become old as clothing becomes old.
You will change them like a coat. And they will be changed,
but You are always the same. Your years will never end.*
PSALM 102:25–27

Life is always changing, and sometimes we appreciate
that fact and sometimes we don't. What's something you
wish could always stay the same? Maybe summer vacation
every day of the year? What's something that you're glad
always changes? Maybe the lunch menu at school? No matter
what changes around us, though, it's so good to know that
God is constantly the same. We depend on Him to be steady
and strong and true, and when we look to Him to guide us,
then we too can be steady and strong and true!

*Dear God, I'm glad You never change and especially
glad that Your love and care for me never change.
Please keep helping and guiding me. Amen.*

THE VERY BEST PROMISE KEEPER

"God is not a man, that He should lie. He is not a son of man, that He should be sorry for what He has said. Has He said, and will He not do it? Has He spoken, and will He not keep His Word?"
NUMBERS 23:19

Think of a time someone made a promise to you and then couldn't keep it. You can probably think of a time when you let someone down that way too. But God will never let anyone down that way. He is the only One who can make a perfect promise. He is the very best at keeping a promise. He is not human, and He cannot lie or make mistakes. When He speaks, His Word is always right and true. Even the very best people who love you the most will let you down sometimes, even if they don't mean to—because they are human. But God is above and beyond us, and you can trust Him completely.

Dear God, thank You for being the very best Promise Keeper! I want to keep reading Your Word and learning more about all of Your extraordinary promises. Amen.

EXTRAORDINARY JOY

*"I have loved you just as My Father has loved Me.
Stay in My love. If you obey My teaching, you will
live in My love. In this way, I have obeyed My Father's
teaching and live in His love. I have told you these things
so My joy may be in you and your joy may be full."*
JOHN 15:9–11

The world around us tries to sell us all kinds of ideas about what real love and joy are. But Jesus tells us here in John 15 how to have real and extraordinary love and joy. When we obey Jesus the way Jesus obeyed God the Father, we stay close to God. And because God is love (see 1 John 4:8), our whole lives are lived in love. When we live in love, we can't help but be full of joy because we are living exactly the way God intended when He created us!

🌸 🌸 🌸

*Dear Jesus, I'm sorry for the times I don't obey You.
Every time I disobey, I want to realize my mistake
and come back to You to get on the right track again.
I want to live in Your love and be full of joy! Amen.*

THE WORK OF GOD'S HAND: PART 1

And yet, O Lord, you are our Father. We are the clay,
and you are the potter. We all are formed by your hand.
ISAIAH 64:8 NLT

Do you remember drawing something or sculpting something out of clay when you were younger, and you knew exactly what it was meant to be, but no one else seemed to? That's because you were the creator, so of course you knew, even if no one else could see it. Never forget that the one true God is your Creator. Sometimes you might not be sure exactly who you are meant to be as you grow up, but God always knows. Keep following Him and asking Him to guide you into the extraordinary life He made you for, full of the good things He has planned for you.

❁ ❁ ❁

Dear God, thank You for making me and having good
plans for me. Please show me step by step what those
plans are. I want to follow You all my days! Amen.

THE WORK OF GOD'S HAND:
PART 2

For You made the parts inside me. You put me together inside my mother. I will give thanks to You, for the greatness of the way I was made brings fear. Your works are great and my soul knows it very well. My bones were not hidden from You when I was made in secret and put together with care in the deep part of the earth. Your eyes saw me before I was put together. And all the days of my life were written in Your book before any of them came to be.

PSALM 139:13–16

This psalm talks about how God planned every detail of you as you grew inside your mother's tummy. He knew every day of your life before you even began to live it! It's too amazing to fully understand how awesome God is and how He created us in such an extraordinary way. So praise Him and honor Him with the life He has given you, asking Him every day to lead You.

Dear God, wow, it's so cool that You've known all my days even before I started living them. Please lead me and help me to obey You and do the good things You made me for. Amen.

EXTRAORDINARY LIKE ESTHER

*Esther told them to say to Mordecai, "Go, gather together
all the Jews who are in Susa, and have them all go without
food so they can pray better for me. Do not eat or drink
for three days, night or day. I and my women servants will
go without food in the same way. Then I will go in to the king,
which is against the law. And if I die, I die." So Mordecai
went away and did just as Esther had told him.*
ESTHER 4:15–17

If you know the story of Esther in the Bible, you know she had extraordinary courage to help save her people from an evil man in a high royal position in the land of Persia. Take time to read the whole book of Esther, and then anytime you're needing some extra faith and courage, ask God to remind you of Esther's extraordinary faith and courage and how God worked out His good plans to protect His people through her. He can do extraordinary things like that through you too, if you are willing to let Him.

*Dear God, I want to be like Esther,
bold and brave to do the extraordinary
things You have planned for me. Amen.*

EXTRAORDINARY CONTENTMENT

I am not saying I need anything. I have learned to be happy with whatever I have. I know how to get along with little and how to live when I have much. I have learned the secret of being happy at all times. If I am full of food and have all I need, I am happy. If I am hungry and need more, I am happy. I can do all things because Christ gives me the strength.
PHILIPPIANS 4:11–13

Do you know what *contentment* means? It means being happy and satisfied with what you have. It means you're not wanting something more or different than what you already have. God can give you extraordinary contentment when you focus on how you can do anything with Jesus giving you strength. Sometimes in life you might have more than enough, while other times you might feel like you don't have enough, especially when you look around too much and compare what you have with what others have. But when you focus on God and trust that He gives you exactly what you need when you need it, then you can be peaceful and thankful all the time.

Dear Jesus, please help me remember how to have total contentment—by trusting I can do all things because You make me strong to face anything! Amen.

WATERS OF THE SEA

The heavens were made by the Word of the Lord.
All the stars were made by the breath of His mouth.
He gathers the waters of the sea together as in a bag.
He places the waters in store-houses. Let all the earth
fear the Lord. Let all the people of the world honor Him.
PSALM 33:6–8

Have you ever sat on the beach, just staring and thinking how incredibly endless the ocean seems? Yet this psalm describes how God can gather the waters of the sea together as if He were simply putting something in a bag. Our one true God is so huge and powerful, so far beyond what our minds can imagine. Let that truth encourage you every single day— because the same huge and powerful God who gathers up the waters easy-peasy is the same huge and powerful God who can give you extraordinary courage and power for what-ever you are facing today.

🌸 🌸 🌸

Dear God, I am amazed by Your greatness and power!
If You can gather up all the waters of the earth and
control them, I trust that You can gather up all my
worries and fears and take them away from me. I know
You will help me and encourage me. Thank You! Amen.

STRENGTH OF HEART LIKE A LION

*Those who are right with God have
as much strength of heart as a lion.*
PROVERBS 28:1

Wow, you are strong if you have trusted Jesus as your Savior!
Believing in Him as the One who took away your sin when
He died on the cross is what makes you right with God. And
if you believe that and are living for Jesus, you have as much
strength of heart as a lion. Does that mean you can go lift a
car in the air or push a train down the tracks? Probably not
unless God decides He wants you to! But it means your in-
sides and emotions are strong to deal with any hard thing
because you know that real strength comes from God alone.
He is in you through His Holy Spirit. You can face anything
without running away because of His extraordinary power
and love for you.

*Dear God, I trust in Jesus as my Savior from sin,
and I'm so grateful that makes me right with You!
Thank You for making me strong like a lion! Amen.*

IN HIS HANDS

*For I have heard many say things to hurt me. Fear is
on every side. They planned together against me. . . .
But as for me, I trust in You, O Lord. I say, "You
are my God." My times are in Your hands.*
PSALM 31:13–15

Has anyone ever said something mean to you? Or maybe to others about you? Maybe they even tried to make plans to get other people to be mean to you. Ugh, it's awful when that happens! In those times, cry out to God. Ask Him for wisdom and help to deal with your hard situation. Remember that He knows everything that is going on with you. Your times are in His hands, and He is always taking care of you no matter what.

❀ ❀ ❀

*Dear God, thank You that I can trust that my times are
in Your hands. Nothing anyone says or does against me
can ever change the fact that You are my God who holds
me, protects me, and takes good care of me. Amen.*

EXTRAORDINARY LIKE ANNA

*Anna was a woman who spoke God's Word. She
was the daughter of Phanuel of the family group of
Asher. Anna was many years old. She had lived with her
husband seven years after she was married. Her husband
had died and she had lived without a husband eighty-four
years. Yet she did not go away from the house of God. She
served God day and night, praying and going without food
so she could pray better. At that time she came and gave
thanks to God. She told the people in Jerusalem about
Jesus. They were looking for the One to save them from
the punishment of their sins and to set them free.*
LUKE 2:36–38

Anna was a woman of the Bible who, after losing her husband, devoted her life to worshipping and praying to God and speaking His Word in the temple. She was extraordinarily close to God. When Jesus' parents brought Him to the temple as a tiny boy, she praised God and told anyone who would listen that Jesus was truly the promised Savior.

❁ ❁ ❁

*Dear God, help me to remember Anna's example
and share Your Word every chance I get. I want to help
people know that Jesus is our one and only Savior. Amen.*

THE VERY BEST LISTENING EAR

You must watch and keep on praying.
Ephesians 6:18

When you hear of someone who has a listening ear, it means they are easy to talk to and care about hearing what others have to say. Having people like that in your life is a real blessing. Maybe for you the person with the best listening ear is a parent or grandparent or your best friend. Just never forget that the One who has the very *best* listening ear is God. He never gets tired of hearing from you in prayer. Any time of day or night, no matter where you are or what you're doing, tell God about everything and ask for His help. Praise Him for who He is and everything He does for you. When you remember He is constantly with you, you can just chatter away in your mind telling Him everything about anything, and He loves it!

❁ ❁ ❁

Dear God, You truly do have the best listening ear!
It's amazing You never tire of hearing from me or anyone who calls on You. Thank You for loving and listening so well! Amen.

LISTEN!

Make your ear open to wisdom. . . . For the Lord gives wisdom. Much learning and understanding come from His mouth. He stores up perfect wisdom for those who are right with Him. He is a safe-covering to those who are right in their walk. He watches over the right way, and He keeps safe the way of those who belong to Him. Then you will understand what is right and good, and right from wrong, and you will know what you should do. For wisdom will come into your heart. And much learning will be pleasing to your soul.
PROVERBS 2:2, 6–10

Since God has such a wonderful listening ear, be sure you are listening well to Him too. The best way to do that is by reading His Word, the Bible. Try hard to read it every day and listen to what God has to say. Ask Him to speak directly to you in whatever you might be going through. And listen to trusted grown-ups and pastors and leaders at church who show in their lives that they trust in Jesus as their Savior and follow Him and love to obey God. Then be open to God speaking to you in extraordinary ways!

Dear God, please help me to remember how incredibly important it is to listen to You! I want to hear Your voice and follow Your ways because that's the very best way to live. Amen.

GOD SPEAKS IN EXTRAORDINARY WAYS

The Angel of the Lord showed Himself to Moses in a burning fire from inside a bush. Moses looked and saw that the bush was burning with fire, but it was not being burned up. So Moses said, "I must step aside and see this great thing, why the bush is not being burned up." The Lord saw him step aside to look. And God called to him from inside the bush, saying, "Moses, Moses!" Moses answered, "Here I am."

EXODUS 3:2–4

God can talk to you through anything in any kind of situation, like the extraordinary way He spoke to Moses through a burning bush. No one can know exactly why God chooses certain incredible ways to speak to His people, but it's just amazing to know He can! Listen to Him first and regularly through reading all of His Word, and also ask Him to speak to you in any kind of way He chooses. Let your heart and mind be open to hearing His voice!

Dear God, thank You for Your Word and the extraordinary ways You speak to Your people. Please speak to me and help me always to listen well. Amen.

A TALKING DONKEY?

*The Lord opened the mouth of the donkey, and she said
to Balaam, "What have I done to you? Why have you hit
me these three times?" Balaam said to the donkey, "Because
you have made a fool of me! If there had been a sword in my
hand, I would have killed you by now!" The donkey said to
Balaam, "Am I not your donkey on which you have traveled
all your life to this day? Have I ever done this to you before?"
And Balaam said, "No." Then the Lord opened Balaam's eyes,
and he saw the angel of the Lord standing in the way with
his sword in his hand. And he bowed to the ground.*
NUMBERS 22:28–31

Another example of God speaking in an extraordinary way
is this story about a donkey speaking to Balaam. Talking
animals usually just show up in fairy tales and movies. But
this was for real, to accomplish the plans God had! God can
speak through anyone or anything and do absolutely any
amazing thing He chooses to!

*Wow, God, it would be so cool if You spoke to me through an
animal like You did for Balaam! But even if You never do,
it's just amazing to know You can. Help me to listen to
You in any way You choose to speak to me. Amen.*

IN THE SIMPLE THINGS

A strong wind tore through the mountains and broke the rocks in pieces before the Lord. But the Lord was not in the wind. After the wind the earth shook. But the Lord was not in the shaking of the earth. After the earth shook, a fire came. But the Lord was not in the fire. And after the fire came a sound of gentle blowing. When Elijah heard it, he put his coat over his face, and went out and stood at the opening of the hole. Then a voice came to him and said, "What are you doing here, Elijah?"
1 KINGS 19:11–13

Sometimes when we're hoping for and expecting God to speak to us or act in an amazing and mighty way, He chooses to surprise us in an extraordinarily simple way instead. Like in this story in 1 Kings, when God let Elijah experience a powerful wind and earthquake and fire. But then the way God actually showed Himself to Elijah was through a gentle breeze. Be listening for God in even the simplest things in your life.

Dear God, please help me to hear You even in totally simple ways if You choose to speak to me that way. Please keep me close to You and always able to hear Your voice! Amen.

EXTRAORDINARY LIKE RAHAB

He said to them, "Go and spy out the land, and Jericho."
So they went and came to the house of Rahab.

JOSHUA 2:1

If you read about Rahab in the Bible, you will learn how she had extraordinary courage to help two men whom Joshua (the leader of the Israelite people after Moses died) sent into the land of Canaan to spy on the city of Jericho. The men came to her house, but then someone found out and warned the king that they were spies. So Rahab helped the two spies hide to protect them. And she told them that she trusted in their God and asked them to help protect her family when they came into the land of Canaan to take it over. The spies promised to help protect Rahab and her family as long as she did not tell anyone about their plans. Then Rahab let them down by a rope through the window and told them to hide for three days in the hill country before returning home. Later, by that same red rope, the spies knew where to find her and her family to protect them from being killed when the Israelites took over Jericho.

🌼 🌼 🌼

Dear God, please help me to remember
Rahab's extraordinary courage to
trust You and help others. Amen.

EXTRAORDINARY ENERGY

Have you not known? Have you not heard? The God Who lives
forever is the Lord, the One Who made the ends of the earth.
He will not become weak or tired. His understanding is too
great for us to begin to know. He gives strength to the weak.
And He gives power to him who has little strength. Even very
young men get tired and become weak and strong young men
trip and fall. But they who wait upon the Lord will get new
strength. They will rise up with wings like eagles. They will run
and not get tired. They will walk and not become weak.
ISAIAH 40:28–31

You've probably heard of some athletes being called a
GOAT—the greatest of all time. But even the very best
"goats" get tired and need their sleep. They don't have endless energy and strength, no matter how much they run
and lift weights and train. Only God never becomes tired or
weak, and this scripture in Isaiah can encourage you when you
do feel tired and weak. Pray to Him and wait for Him. He is
your source of true energy and strength.

Dear God, thank You that even though I get tired
and weak, You never do, and You give me new
energy and strength exactly when I need it. Amen.

THE ONE WHO HAS ALL POWER

At the right time, we will be shown that God is the One Who has all power. He is the King of kings and Lord of lords. He can never die. He lives in a light so bright that no man can go near Him. No man has ever seen God or can see Him. Honor and power belong to Him forever.
1 TIMOTHY 6:15–16

No one yet has ever fully seen God because He is so awesome and extraordinary that we humans just aren't able. It's a little like trying to look at the sun. We know the sun is there and we can see it and all the good it does, but it's just not possible for our human eyes to look at it directly because it's just too much! Our eyes were not made to look at something so bright. But someday, at just the right time, the Bible tells us, we will get to see God fully, and we will see how awesome and powerful He is over everything in all creation.

☘ ☘ ☘

Dear God, even now on earth while I can't fully see You, I trust that You are working and guiding me. And it's so cool to know that one day I will see You fully! I love You! Amen.

EXTRAORDINARY PEACE

The peace of God is much greater than the
human mind can understand. This peace will
keep your hearts and minds through Christ Jesus.
PHILIPPIANS 4:7

Sometimes life might feel super stressful. Maybe schoolwork is extra hard these days, or maybe you just started a new school. Maybe you or a loved one is really sick and need a lot of medical care. Maybe there's a lot of conflict in your home. But no matter what is going on, God can give you extraordinary peace. If you focus on all the stress, of course you will be stressed. So focus instead on what Philippians 4 goes on to say: "Keep your minds thinking about whatever is true, whatever is respected, whatever is right, whatever is pure, whatever can be loved, and whatever is well thought of. If there is anything good and worth giving thanks for, think about these things. Keep on doing all the things you learned and received and heard from me. Do the things you saw me do. Then the God Who gives peace will be with you" (Philippians 4:8–9).

Dear God, help me to trust You in the middle of stress
and stay focused on what is good and right and true.
I know You are with me and helping me in every hard
thing and will give me Your awesome peace. Amen.

47

HONOR HIM FOREVER

God's riches are so great! The things He knows and His wisdom are so deep! No one can understand His thoughts. No one can understand His ways. The Holy Writings say, "Who knows the mind of the Lord? Who is able to tell Him what to do?" "Who has given first to God, that God should pay him back?" Everything comes from Him. His power keeps all things together. All things are made for Him. May He be honored forever.
ROMANS 11:33–36

This scripture reminds you how truly extraordinary and awesome God is! No one can ever fully understand Him. Does that mean we shouldn't even try? No way! He shows so much of Himself to us through His Word, through His creation, through His people, and on and on! Everything comes from Him and is made for Him and is held together by His great power. He wants us to keep on getting to know Him and His amazing love for us.

Dear God, I worship You! You are truly extraordinary, awesome, and amazing! I want to take time every day to focus on how wonderful You are! Amen.

TAKE GOOD CARE

Do you not know that your body is a house of God where the Holy Spirit lives? God gave you His Holy Spirit. Now you belong to God. You do not belong to yourselves. God bought you with a great price. So honor God with your body. You belong to Him.
1 CORINTHIANS 6:19–20

Choose now while you are young to always remember how extraordinary you are as a child of God and take good care of yourself! Ask God every day to help you make healthy and wise choices, because if you have asked Jesus to be your Savior, the Holy Spirit lives in you—and that makes your body a house for the Holy Spirit! The Bible says you are not your own but you belong to God. That's a good thing—the very best thing, actually!—because no one loves or cares for you like God does.

☼ ☼ ☼

Dear God, thank You that I belong to You! Thank You for living in me! Please help me to take care of my body the best I can so that as You live in me I can do the good things You have planned for me. Amen.

EXTRAORDINARY MISSIONARIES

*"You will tell about Me in the city of Jerusalem
and over all the countries of Judea and
Samaria and to the ends of the earth."*
ACTS 1:8

Think about a country you'd love to visit and why. Do you
think it would be cool to learn about the culture and the people there? There are so many different customs and traditions
among the unique people God created! But a lot of those
customs and traditions have nothing to do with the one true
God and our Savior, Jesus Christ. With respect and kindness,
we should lovingly share about the Bible and Jesus with people from all cultures. One of the best ways we can do that is
by supporting missionaries who make it their goal to go and
live in foreign countries to share the good news about Jesus.
These extraordinary people bravely teach others about God's
love. Pray for them and ask God to show you how best to
support them.

*Dear God, thank You for amazing missionaries
who share Your love and truth all over the world!
Please help them and show me how to help them. Amen.*

WHERE YOUR HELP COMES FROM

I will lift up my eyes to the mountains. Where will my help come from? My help comes from the Lord, Who made heaven and earth. He will not let your feet go out from under you. He Who watches over you will not sleep. Listen, He Who watches over Israel will not close his eyes or sleep. The Lord watches over you. The Lord is your safe cover at your right hand. The sun will not hurt you during the day and the moon will not hurt you during the night. The Lord will keep you from all that is sinful. He will watch over your soul. The Lord will watch over your coming and going, now and forever.

PSALM 121:1–8

Throughout your life, you'll need to ask for help with a lot of different things, and it's good to remember that every bit of help you get ultimately comes from God. He is the One watching over you at all times and providing the people and things you need when you need them. Praise and thank Him every time you ask for help and receive it and for all the ways you are helped without ever even having to ask!

Dear God, I can never thank You enough for the bazillion ways You help me all the time. You are so good and loving! Amen.

EXTRAORDINARY LIKE SHIPHRAH AND PUAH

*Then the king of Egypt spoke to the Hebrew nurses.
The name of one was Shiphrah. The name of the other
was Puah. He said, "When you are helping the Hebrew
women to give birth, and see the baby before the mother
does, if it is a son, kill him. But if it is a daughter, let her
live." But the nurses feared God. They did not do what
the king of Egypt told them. They let the boys live.*
EXODUS 1:15–17

When Pharaoh, the Egyptian king, ordered that every new
baby boy born to God's people was to be killed, two of the
nurses who helped moms as they delivered their babies chose
to respect God instead of Pharaoh. They secretly defied
Pharaoh and refused to kill the baby boys. These women
were named Shiphrah and Puah, and we can follow their courageous example of extraordinary respect for God and love
for others, even when it was so dangerous for them to defy
the king.

❀ ❀ ❀

*Dear God, help me to have great respect for You
plus courage and love for others, especially the
smallest among us, just like Shiphrah and Puah
did to save the lives of the Israelite baby boys. Amen.*

EXTRAORDINARY LIKE JOCHEBED

The time came when she could hide him no longer.
So she took a basket made from grass, and covered
it with tar and put the child in it. And she set it in
the grass by the side of the Nile. His sister stayed
to watch and find out what would happen to him.

EXODUS 2:3–4

One of the Israelite babies Shiphrah and Puah saved was Moses, and his mother's name was Jochebed. When it got harder and harder for her to keep hiding baby Moses as he grew bigger, she showed extraordinary courage and clever thinking. She came up with a plan to put Moses in a basket in the river near where the Egyptian princess liked to bathe. Jochebed hoped that the princess would find Moses and take care of him and keep him safe from the evil Pharaoh who wanted to kill all baby boys. And that's exactly what happened! Moses was safe and could grow up to be the great leader God planned for him to be!

🌸 🌸 🌸

Dear God, please help me to have courage and
think in clever ways, just like Jochebed. Amen.

EXTRAORDINARY LIKE MIRIAM

*His sister said to Pharaoh's daughter, "Should I go
and call a nurse from the Hebrew women to nurse
the child for you?" Pharaoh's daughter said to her,
"Go." So the girl went and called the child's mother.*
EXODUS 2:7–8

Maybe you've had to help watch over younger siblings, but probably not quite like Miriam in the Bible did. After her mother, Jochebed, came up with the idea to put baby Moses in a little basket in the river near where the Egyptian princess liked to bathe, Miriam helped make sure baby Moses stayed safe. She was the one to bravely speak up when the princess discovered Moses. Miriam asked the princess if she wanted her to find someone to feed the baby until he was old enough to eat on his own and then go live with the princess. Her courageous action helped save Moses' life, plus he got to stay with his family a little longer! Miriam truly did an extraordinary job watching over her baby brother.

*Dear God, please help me to do a good
job looking out for those younger than
me whenever I am needed. Amen.*

ALWAYS EVERYWHERE

Where can I go from Your Spirit? Or where can I run away from where You are? If I go up to heaven, You are there! If I make my bed in the place of the dead, You are there! If I take the wings of the morning or live in the farthest part of the sea, even there Your hand will lead me and Your right hand will hold me.

PSALM 139:7–10

God is so extraordinary, He is *omnipresent*. That's a big word meaning He is in all places all the time. Everywhere you go, He is with you. In good times and bad, He is right there, and you can call out to Him for help or in worship or just to talk to Him about anything. No person can ever promise you what God promises you. He says, "I will never leave you or let you be alone" (Hebrews 13:5).

Dear God, thank You for being in all places all the time. I sure need You with me every moment, and I'm so grateful You never leave me. Amen.

55

WE BELONG TO GOD

We know that we belong to God, but the whole world is under the power of the devil. We know God's Son has come. He has given us the understanding to know Him Who is the true God. We are joined together with the true God through His Son, Jesus Christ. He is the true God and the life that lasts forever. My children, keep yourselves from false gods.
1 JOHN 5:19–21

You might wonder sometimes why bad things happen in this world. It's because the whole world is under the power of the devil. But for all of us who believe in Jesus as Savior, we belong to God and the devil can never defeat us. The devil can attack us and hurt us, but God gives us life that lasts forever, no matter what! We should never want to follow any type of false god who will lead us into the ways of the devil. Only the one true God leads us to life that lasts forever.

Dear God, please show me and protect me from everything that is bad and help me to keep myself away from false gods. I trust that with Jesus as my Savior, no matter what happens to me, You give me life that lasts forever! Amen.

EXTRAORDINARY GOALS

I will be careful to live a life without blame. When will You come to me? I will walk within my house with a right and good heart. I will set no sinful thing in front of my eyes. I hate the work of those who are not faithful. It will not get hold of me. A sinful heart will be far from me. I will have nothing to do with sin.

PSALM 101:2–4

It's not popular in this world to say you will have nothing to do with sin. A lot of people would say that's no fun and that it's no big deal to play around a little with bad choices. So it's an extraordinary goal to say like this verse that you want nothing to do with sin. And it's a very good goal. Jesus took all sin away from us when He died on the cross, and that is grace, but now we should never want to sin or act like bad things are no big deal. Because Jesus had to die to save us from sin, we should think about how serious and awful sin is and want to avoid it as much as possible.

✿ ✿ ✿

Dear God, please show me every day the sins I need to get rid of in my life. I don't ever want to play around with them. When I mess up, I trust that You forgive me because of Jesus, and I am grateful! Amen.

KEEP ON ASKING

Jesus told them a picture-story to show that men should always pray and not give up. He said, "There was a man in one of the cities who was head of the court. His work was to say if a person was guilty or not. This man was not afraid of God. He did not respect any man. In that city there was a woman whose husband had died. She kept coming to him and saying, 'Help me! There is someone who is working against me.' For awhile he would not help her. Then he began to think, 'I am not afraid of God and I do not respect any man. But I will see that this woman whose husband has died gets her rights because I get tired of her coming all the time.' " Then the Lord said, "Listen to the words of the sinful man who is head of the court. Will not God make the things that are right come to His chosen people who cry day and night to Him?"

LUKE 18:1–7

Jesus gave us this example of a woman being persistent to teach us to be persistent too. The point is that if a judge in the courts who did not even respect God was finally willing to help the woman who kept asking and asking, how much more will God help His people who keep asking for His help?

🌼 🌼 🌼

Dear God, thank You that You want me to keep on asking and asking and asking for Your help! Amen.

EXTRAORDINARY TRANSFORMATION

At once Saul began to preach in the Jewish places of worship that Jesus is the Son of God. All who heard him were surprised and wondered. They said, "This is the man who beat and killed the followers in Jerusalem. He came here to tie the followers in chains and take them to the head religious leaders." But Saul kept on growing in power. The Jews living in Damascus wondered about Saul's preaching. He was proving that Jesus was the Christ.
ACTS 9:20–22

Saul in the Bible, who was also known as Paul, went through a total and extraordinary transformation. God changed him completely! He went from killing Christians who believed in Jesus to becoming a Christian himself and preaching about Jesus so others would believe in Him. When people saw that extraordinary change in Saul's life, it made them pay attention with surprise and wonder, and it helped prove to many people that Jesus is exactly who He says He is.

✿ ✿ ✿

Dear God, thank You for examples of extraordinary transformation. You are able to change anyone's heart and mind to believe in You and live for You! That's so cool! Please do that in the lives of these people I'm praying for: _____. Amen.

EXTRAORDINARY CREATOR

*"For in six days the Lord made the heavens,
the earth, the sea and all that is in them."*
Exodus 20:11

God sure is an incredible, extraordinary Creator! Only He could create the whole world and everything in it! The cool thing is, He gave us creative abilities too—not exactly the same as His, but we are made in His image and able to be creative in our own human ways. So ask God to show you all the unique talents and gifts He has given you. Ask Him to show you how to use them creatively. Then get started using those gifts to bring glory to God and help others come to know Him and trust in Jesus as Savior.

*Dear God, Your creation is so incredibly cool! You are
the one true awesome Creator, and anything I can
create is a gift from You! Help me to be creative
in the good ways You want me to be. Amen.*

KNOW-IT-ALL

"For I am God, and there is no other. I am God, and there is no one like Me. I tell from the beginning what will happen in the end. And from times long ago I tell of things which have not been done, saying, 'My Word will stand. And I will do all that pleases Me.'... I have planned it, and I will do it."
ISAIAH 46:9–11

God is so extraordinary that He knows absolutely everything. He's truly the one and only Know-It-All, and that's a good thing! Another way to describe His complete knowledge is with the word *omniscient*. Scripture tells us that God can tell from the beginning what will happen in the end. Sometimes we wish He would tell us everything He knows, but He wants us to trust Him day by day. He has good plans, and our job is to love and follow and worship and serve Him until one day we are in heaven with Him forever.

Dear God, You know everything! You always have and always will. I trust Your goodness and Your plans! Please help me to keep on following You day by day. Amen.

EXTRAORDINARY RACE

Let us put every thing out of our lives that keeps us from doing what we should. Let us keep running in the race that God has planned for us. Let us keep looking to Jesus. Our faith comes from Him and He is the One Who makes it perfect.
HEBREWS 12:1–2

The Bible says God has a race just for you! He has planned the course of your life, and if you keep looking to Jesus, He will lead you on it. As you keep looking to Him, you also have to constantly get rid of anything in your life that tries to pull you away from following Him. So it's super important to keep reading the Bible and learning from others who love and follow Jesus—at church and in your family and friendships.

Dear Jesus, I want to keep looking to You every day. Please keep me on the good course You have set for me in this race of life You have planned for me. Please keep growing and strengthening my faith in You! Amen.

EXTRAORDINARY HELPER

God has said, "I will never leave you or let you be alone."
So we can say for sure, "The Lord is my Helper. I am
not afraid of anything man can do to me."
HEBREWS 13:5–6

In any scary situation, it helps to have someone with you, right? But if no other person is around, the scary situation seems even worse. That's why it's so important to remember that you are never, ever, *ever* totally alone. God has promised that He *never* leaves you! He is your Helper at all times. You might have family and friends who love you and love to help you, but no person can promise what God promises! You can trust Him and call out to Him in any kind of trouble—day or night, no matter where you are—and be confident that He is more powerful than anything that could happen to you. He loves and rescues you!

Dear God, thank You for being my constant
Helper. Please help me remember that
You are always with me. Amen.

STORY OF A SERVANT GIRL: PART 1

One day as we were going to the place to pray, we met a servant-girl who could tell what was going to happen in the future by a demon she had. Her owner made much money from her power. She followed Paul and us crying out, "These are servants of the Highest God. They are telling you how to be saved from the punishment of sin." She did this many days. Paul was troubled. Then he turned and said to the demon in her, "In the name of Jesus Christ, I speak to you. Come out of her!" At once it left her.

Acts 16:16–18

This poor servant girl in the Bible had a demon inside her that told the future, and her owners were making money off her. When she met Paul, the demon inside her made her follow Paul and his friends and pester and provoke them over and over. But because of the power of Jesus working through Paul, he was able to command the demon to come out of the girl and stop controlling her.

Dear Jesus, thank You for Your extraordinary power working through people to rescue them from evil spirits. I pray that You would keep working Your power to rescue people who need it every day, and please show me how I can help! Amen.

STORY OF A SERVANT GIRL: PART 2

The girl's owners saw that they could not make money with her anymore. Then they took hold of Paul and Silas and dragged them to the leaders. This happened in the center of town where people gather.

Acts 16:19

If you read on in the story about the servant girl, you find that her owners were very angry that Paul had commanded the demon to leave her. Paul had just made them lose out on a lot of money they could have made from the girl! This event kicked off a series of events that put Paul and his friend Silas in jail. But then God worked an extraordinary miracle to free Paul and Silas and save the life of the jailer, as well as help the jailer and all his family to trust in Jesus as Savior.

Dear God, You are working through all kinds of unexpected circumstances and in all kinds of extraordinary ways to bring people to saving faith in You! Your love for people is amazing! Amen.

ALWAYS STRONGER

*The One Who lives in you is stronger
than the one who is in the world.*
1 JOHN 4:4

This is such a simple and powerful scripture to memorize and repeat when you need extraordinary courage in any situation. Our enemy the devil is the one stirring up all kinds of evil in this world. And you will be under attack from him sometimes, in all sorts of different ways—through someone else's unkind words or actions, through stressful times for your family, through painful times of loss, through sickness, and on and on. But no matter how strong the enemy and his evil seem against you and your loved ones, they are never stronger than the power of God in you through the Holy Spirit. Don't ever forget that. Call on God to help you be strong and calm and patient and to help you see how He is working and taking care of you through it all.

*Dear God, deep down I know You are always stronger
than any evil attack against me, any hard thing I'm
going through. But I do forget that truth sometimes,
and I'm sorry. Please remind me and fill me with Your
power and peace and do the fighting for me. Amen.*

EXTRAORDINARY EYES

The eyes of the Lord are in every place,
watching the bad and the good.
PROVERBS 15:3

No one has vision like God does. The Bible says He sees and knows everything that happens in every place. "No one can hide from God. His eyes see everything we do. We must give an answer to God for what we have done," says Hebrews 4:13. And Job 28:24 says, "He looks to the ends of the earth, and sees everything under the heavens." For people making bad choices, those verses might be scary, but for those who love God and want to follow and obey His Word, they are wonderful and encouraging. God only wants you to obey His good ways because He loves you and wants what's best for you. When you trust that He always sees you, you can have peace and courage, knowing He's able to help in every moment.

🌸 🌸 🌸

Dear God, please remind me that You are always
watching me—in every place and every moment.
Let this truth encourage me! Amen.

EXTRAORDINARY PROTECTION

At my first trial no one helped me. Everyone left me. I hope this will not be held against them. But the Lord was with me. He gave me power to preach the Good News so all the people who do not know God might hear. I was taken from the mouth of the lion. The Lord will look after me and will keep me from every sinful plan they have. He will bring me safe into His holy nation of heaven. May He have all the shining-greatness forever.
2 Timothy 4:16–18

Even when Paul had no one else to help, God Himself was with Paul and gave him power. Paul trusted that God would protect him from every sinful plan that any bad people might have. And he knew God would someday bring him into heaven forever. Paul wrote these things in his letter to Timothy, but they are true for you today as well. God gives His people extraordinary protection!

Dear God, thank You for keeping me safe from any bad plans for me. I trust that no matter what happens here in this world, You will ultimately always keep me safe because someday You are going to bring me into perfect paradise in heaven with You! Amen.

AWESOME ANSWER

"Where were you when I began building the earth?
Tell Me, if you have understanding. Who decided how big
it was to be, since you know? Who looked to see if it was
as big as it should be? What was it built upon? Who laid its
first stone, when the morning stars sang together and all
the sons of God called out for joy? Who shut up the sea
with doors, when it rushed out from its secret place?"
JOB 38:4–8

Do grown-ups in your life ever ask you questions that they
know you know the answers to? They do it as a reminder. In
this passage, God is asking Job some questions that He knows
Job knows the answers to. God is asking as a reminder to Job
that God alone is incredible, all-powerful, amazing, and every
other awesome adjective. Only the one true God has extraordinary power to create and control all things. Whether your
life is feeling hard or feeling wonderful, worship God today
and every day. Trust Him with your life, because He alone is
able to do anything!

Dear God, You are the awesome answer to every question
about who creates and has power and does all good things!
I am so blessed to know and worship You! Amen.

EXTRAORDINARY LIKE ABIGAIL

The man's name was Nabal, and his wife's name was
Abigail. The woman was of good understanding and
beautiful. But the man was bad and sinful in his ways.
1 Samuel 25:3

Not long before David became king of Israel, there was a man named Nabal who was very rich. His wife's name was Abigail, and she was beautiful, kind, and wise. Nabal, on the other hand, was foolish and sinful in all of his ways. In the past, David had helped protect the men who worked for Nabal. When David and his men set up camp near where Nabal and his men were working, David sent some of his men to go to Nabal to ask him for food and supplies. David had been kind to Nabal's men, and he figured Nabal would be kind in return. But Nabal would not share anything. His refusal to help made David so angry that he was ready to fight and kill.

One of Nabal's men went to Abigail to tell her what had happened. Right away, Abigail sent plenty of food and drink to David and his men. When Abigail met up with them, she begged David not to act in anger toward Nabal's men because of Nabal's selfishness. David thanked her and listened to her. Nabal acted in foolishness, and David nearly overreacted in great anger. But Abigail acted in wisdom and generosity and saved many lives.

Dear God, please help me to be a wise
and generous peacemaker like Abigail. Amen.

WHAT KIND OF MAN IS HE?

*On one of those days Jesus and His followers got into
a boat. Jesus said to them, "Let us go over to the other
side of the lake." Then they pushed out into the water.
As they were going, Jesus fell asleep. A wind storm came
over the lake. The boat was filling with water and they were
in danger. The followers came to awake Jesus. They said,
"Teacher! Teacher! We are going to die!" Then Jesus got up and
spoke sharp words to the wind and the high waves. The wind
stopped blowing and there were no more waves. He said to
them, "Where is your faith?" The followers were surprised and
afraid. They said to each other, "What kind of a man is He?
He speaks to the wind and the waves and they obey Him."*
Luke 8:22–25

Let this story in the Bible remind you that Jesus can command anything in all creation to obey Him. He could simply
speak words to a storm to make it stop. He has extraordinary
power over everything, and He loves and cares for *you*. Let
this truth fill you with courage to face any hard thing.

🌸 🌸 🌸

*Dear God, I'm thankful all things obey You, and You
can do anything at all to protect and help me. I feel
loved and safe because You take care of me. Amen.*

71

SAFE PLACE

My soul is quiet and waits for God alone. My hope comes from Him. He alone is my rock and the One Who saves me. He is my strong place. I will not be shaken. My being safe and my honor rest with God. My safe place is in God, the rock of my strength. Trust in Him at all times, O people. Pour out your heart before Him. God is a safe place for us.
PSALM 62:5–8

If you think of your safe place, do you think of the place you feel most comfortable and relaxed and understood? Maybe you think of being at home with your parents, cozy and well taken care of. Or maybe you think of your safe place as with your best friend you can talk to about anything. Those are good safe places, but God wants to be your very best, rock-solid Safe Place! He is with you anytime and anywhere. Talk to Him, cry out to Him, depend on Him, and trust Him for everything you need.

Dear God, please help me to trust You at all times. Thank You that I can pour out my heart to You anytime, anywhere. You are my solid Rock and Safe Place everywhere I go, in every situation. Amen.

EXTRAORDINARY PROVIDER

"Look at the birds in the sky. They do not plant seeds.
They do not gather grain. They do not put grain into a
building to keep. Yet your Father in heaven feeds them! Are
you not more important than the birds? . . . Why should you
worry about clothes? Think how the flowers grow. They do not
work or make cloth. . . . Do not worry. Do not keep saying,
'What will we eat?' or, 'What will we drink?' or, 'What will we
wear?' The people who do not know God are looking for all
these things. Your Father in heaven knows you need all these
things. First of all, look for the holy nation of God. Be right
with Him. All these other things will be given to you also."
MATTHEW 6:26, 28, 31–33

When you trust God, you will always have what you need. He
is an extraordinary Provider! If you are ever worried about
food or clothes or anything, let this scripture from Matthew
6 be your reminder that God takes extraordinarily good care
of you!

Dear God, if the birds trust You, then I sure can too!
Thank You so much that You provide anything and
everything I truly need. I love You! Amen.

OUR HELPER

The Holy Spirit helps us where we are weak. We do not know how to pray or what we should pray for, but the Holy Spirit prays to God for us with sounds that cannot be put into words. God knows the hearts of men. He knows what the Holy Spirit is thinking. The Holy Spirit prays for those who belong to Christ the way God wants Him to pray.
ROMANS 8:26–27

Sometimes you might feel so scared and worried about something that you just don't have a clue how to pray. That's when you have to remember you have an extraordinary Helper—the Holy Spirit—who actually prays for you when you can't find the words. Wow! Thank God for that gift and let it make you brave. God is with you through His Holy Spirit, always knowing everything you need and everything you think. He helps even when you don't know how to ask for help!

Dear God, thank You for giving me Your Holy Spirit as my Helper and for knowing me better than I know myself! Amen.

EXTRAORDINARY FORGIVENESS

He has not punished us enough for all our sins. He has not paid us back for all our wrong-doings. For His loving-kindness for those who fear Him is as great as the heavens are high above the earth. He has taken our sins from us as far as the east is from the west.
PSALM 103:10–12

If a friend does something not so nice to you again and again and again, it can be hard to forgive them, right? So think about how awesome it is that God forgives us like crazy even though we do not-so-nice things a *lot*. Those not-so-nice things are sins, and when we don't acknowledge them and ask for forgiveness, they hurt our friendship with God. But as soon as we admit them and ask God to take them away, He does—as far as the east is from the west, actually. That's super far! And then we draw closer to God and His goodness.

Dear God, no one forgives as well as You do!
I'm grateful, because I need Your forgiveness often.
Remind me always to admit my sins to You and let
You take them far, far away. Thank You! Amen.

EXTRAORDINARY GRACE

*Are we to keep on sinning so that God will give
us more of His loving-favor? No, not at all!*
ROMANS 6:1–2

Since God forgives so fully and so well, sometimes we might
think it's no big deal to keep doing anything we want, even if
it's sinful, and then just ask for forgiveness, since God loves
to forgive. But that's not a good way to think. If we truly
love God, we want to obey Him and honor Him, not choose
bad things again and again with a "who cares?" attitude. We
are for sure going to mess up and make bad choices, but
we should feel sad about that and how it hurts God and then
do our best to avoid more sin in the future. Also, even though
God always forgives when we ask, He doesn't always keep us
from the consequences that often go along with sin. Ask God
to help you keep running away from sin; don't play around
with it like it doesn't matter.

*Dear God, thank You for Your extraordinary grace.
Knowing You love and forgive me time and time again
gives me courage. But I don't want to purposefully sin
against You or pretend it's no big deal. Please help me
to keep getting better at turning away from sin. Amen.*

EXTRAORDINARY LIKE SAMSON'S MOM

*There was a certain man of Zorah. . . . His name was
Manoah. His wife was not able to have children. Then the
angel of the Lord came to the woman and said to her, "See,
you have not been able to have any children. But the Lord
will make it possible for you to have a child and you will give
birth to a son. So be careful not to drink wine or strong drink.
Do not eat anything that is unclean. You will have a child
and give birth to a son. His hair must never be cut. Because
the boy will be a Nazirite to God from the time he is born.
He will begin to take Israel away from the Philistines' power."*

JUDGES 13:2–5

We don't know the name of Samson's mom, but we do know
she was given a lot of rules about how to take care of him
right from the very beginning of his life, while he was still in
her tummy. Some people might get upset about being told
how to take care of their own child. But Samson's mom and
dad wanted to obey God's instructions that He sent through
an angel. They even asked God to send the angel again to
make sure they were doing their best to care for Samson exactly the way God wanted. That's extraordinary obedience to
God and a great example to follow.

🌸 🌸 🌸

*Dear God, like Samson's mom, I want to obey You
right down to the tiniest details. Please help me. Amen.*

IMAGINING THE WORST

God is our safe place and our strength. He is always our help when we are in trouble. So we will not be afraid, even if the earth is shaken and the mountains fall into the center of the sea, and even if its waters go wild with storm and the mountains shake with its action.

PSALM 46:1–3

As a kid, you probably have a great big imagination! That's wonderful most of the time! But sometimes it's bad if you let your imagination run wild thinking of and worrying about scary things that could happen but probably never will. Let this scripture remind you that even the craziest-sounding awful thing you can think of that might happen—like the mountains falling into the center of the sea (yikes!)—never needs to scare you because God is your Safe Place and Strength. He is always ready and able to help you in any kind of trouble.

✿ ✿ ✿

Dear God, You are mighty and awesome, more powerful than any awful thing I can imagine. You are my help and safety in any kind of trouble. Thank You! Amen.

SHOW ME LOVING-KINDNESS

*Show me loving-kindness, O Lord, for I
am in trouble. My eyes, my soul and my
body are becoming weak from being sad.*
PSALM 31:9

Many things in life can make you feel sad sometimes. You might just want to cry and cry! Maybe you've gotten yourself into trouble and you're not sure how to get out. Maybe someone is being mean to you all the time at school. Maybe you can't understand your homework and it just seems way too hard. Maybe a loved one has died or a close friend has moved away. In those times when you feel like you'll never stop crying, be sure to cry out to God. Ask Him for more of His loving-kindness. This psalm goes on to say to God, "How great is Your loving-kindness! You have stored it up for those who fear You. You show it to those who trust in You" (Psalm 31:19).

🌼 🌼 🌼

*Dear God, I trust You and Your loving-kindness. I trust that
You want to give me more and more of it, especially when
I'm feeling sad. Please show me that You care about my
sadness, and give me help and comfort to get through it. Amen.*

EXTRAORDINARY BEAUTY

*Do not let your beauty come from the outside. It should
not be the way you comb your hair or the wearing of gold
or the wearing of fine clothes. Your beauty should come
from the inside. It should come from the heart. This is the
kind that lasts. Your beauty should be a gentle and quiet
spirit. In God's sight this is of great worth and no amount of
money can buy it. This was the kind of beauty seen in the holy
women who lived many years ago. They put their hope in God.*
1 PETER 3:3–5

No matter what anyone tries to tell you or what social media
photos try to show you, real and extraordinary beauty comes
from the inside, not what anyone looks like on the outside.
Your heart—the way you treat others and share kindness and
love—is what makes you truly gorgeous. If you have a gentle
and quiet spirit, it means you are listening for God's voice and
leading in your life and you put your hope in Him. This kind of
beauty never fades away.

*Dear God, please help me not to focus on outer
appearance but on real inner beauty that shines out
of me and helps others want to know You more! Amen.*

POWER TO HEAL

Jesus came to Peter's house. He saw Peter's wife's mother in bed. She was very sick. He touched her hand and the sickness left her. She got up and cared for Jesus. That evening they brought to Jesus many people who had demons in them. The demons were put out when Jesus spoke to them. All the sick people were healed. It happened as the early preacher Isaiah said it would happen. He said, "He took on Himself our sickness and carried away our diseases."
MATTHEW 8:14–17

When Jesus was on earth, He showed that He truly was God through His extraordinary power to heal people of sickness and demons. And He proved true what early preachers like Isaiah had said to show that He was the Savior the Jewish people had been waiting and hoping for.

Dear Jesus, I believe You are truly God! You have the power to heal and perform any miracle. You are awesome, and I praise You! Amen.

THIS IS LOVE!

*Dear friends, let us love each other, because love comes
from God. Those who love are God's children and they
know God. Those who do not love do not know God because
God is love. God has shown His love to us by sending His
only Son into the world. God did this so we might have life
through Christ. This is love! It is not that we loved God but
that He loved us. For God sent His Son to pay for our sins
with His own blood. Dear friends, if God loved us that much,
then we should love each other. No person has ever seen
God at any time. If we love each other, God lives in us.
His love is made perfect in us. He has given us His Spirit.
This is how we live by His help and He lives in us.*
1 JOHN 4:7–13

God's love is the only kind of real love. It is truly extraordinary, and we are called to share it with others—but not on our
own. God lives in us through His Spirit and helps us share it!

*Dear God, You are real and extraordinary love!
Please keep living in me and helping me share it! Amen.*

EXTRAORDINARY LIKE THE POOR WIDOW

*A poor woman whose husband had died came
by and gave two very small pieces of money.*
MARK 12:42

One day Jesus sat down near where people put money for offerings to God. Jesus watched as many rich people gave large amounts of money. Their giving wasn't hard for them to do because they were so rich that they had plenty of money to share. But then Jesus watched one woman, who was terribly poor and had no husband, drop in two very small copper coins. Added together, the two coins weren't even worth one whole cent!

Jesus saw this and said, "This is the truth—this poor widow has given more money than all the others." Really? The widow had given only two small coins that didn't even add up to a penny! And the rich people had given a whole bunch of money—a whole lot more than the poor widow. But Jesus said, "The rich people put in money they didn't even need because they have so much extra. But the poor widow has nothing extra. She needed every bit of her money to live on, but still she gave it all to God" (see Mark 12:43–44).

🌼 🌼 🌼

*Dear God, help me to give in extraordinary ways,
like the poor widow who had such great faith that
she gave absolutely everything she had to You. Amen.*

LISTEN, LEARN, AND DO

"And why do you call Me, 'Lord, Lord,' but do not do what I say? Whoever comes to Me and hears and does what I say, I will show you who he is like. He is like a man who built a house. He dug deep to put the building on rock. When the water came up and the river beat against the house, the building could not be shaken because it was built on rock. But he who hears and does not do what I say, is like a man who built a house on nothing but earth. The water beat against the house. At once it fell and was destroyed."
<small>LUKE 6:46–49</small>

We could read the Bible and hear what Jesus taught all day long, but if we don't do anything with that truth, then we won't stand strong in faith and wisdom during hard times. We'll be like a sandcastle at the beach that gets washed away as soon as any wave hits. But if we actually listen, learn, and do what Jesus taught, we're like a strong house built on solid rock that will be able to handle anything in life that comes our way, in good times and bad.

Dear Jesus, I want to listen, learn, and do all You have to say. Please help me! Amen.

EXTRAORDINARY LIKE JEHOSHEBA

*When Ahaziah's mother Athaliah saw that her son was
dead, she got up and killed all the king's children. But King
Joram's daughter Jehosheba, Ahaziah's sister, took Joash
the son of Ahaziah. She stole him away from the king's sons
who were being killed, and put him and his nurse in the
bedroom. They hid him from Athaliah, and he was not killed.
Joash was hid with his nurse in the house of the Lord six
years, while Athaliah was ruling over the land.*
2 KINGS 11:1–3

Jehosheba was a princess in the Bible who proved how brave
she was when she rescued her young nephew Joash. Queen
Athaliah wanted to kill him, but Jehosheba hid him and his
nurse for six years while the evil queen ruled over the land.
God used Jehosheba's extraordinary courage to ensure that
Joash became the rightful king of Judah.

🌸 🌸 🌸

*Dear God, please help me to remember
the courage of Jehosheba. Use me to
help and protect others too. Amen.*

DREAM HOME

How beautiful are the places where You live, O Lord of all!
My soul wants and even becomes weak from wanting to be
in the house of the Lord. . . . How happy are those who live
in Your house! They are always giving thanks to You.
PSALM 84:1–2, 4

Do you ever think about what your dream house would be like? Maybe you've even drawn a picture of it. And where would your dream house be if you could live anywhere at all? It's fun to imagine! But better than any home we can dream up here on earth is the forever home God is creating for us in heaven. It will be truly extraordinary! And when we take time to focus on God and praise Him and hear from Him through His Word, we get little glimpses of how incredible that perfect forever home will be!

Dear God, thank You for my blessings here and now where
I live on earth, but even more, thank You for the perfect
home in heaven with You that You are making for me! Amen.

EXTRAORDINARY REST

"Come to Me, all of you who work and have heavy loads. I will give you rest. Follow My teachings and learn from Me. I am gentle and do not have pride. You will have rest for your souls."
MATTHEW 11:28–29

The best kind of rest is the kind Jesus gives. It's not like taking a great nap or getting to sleep in or going on an amazing and relaxing vacation. It's even better. It's a way of life that gives you deep peace because you've asked Jesus to be your Savior and you follow Him and learn from Him. Yes, sometimes things in life might still feel stressful or tiring, but turning to Jesus in those times reminds you to slow down and let Him take away the worries as you trust in Him.

Dear Jesus, please help me to breathe deeply and slow down and give You any worries or tiredness I might feel. You give the best kind of rest as I follow You. Amen.

CHOOSING BAPTISM

*Jesus came and said to them, "All power has been given
to Me in heaven and on earth. Go and make followers
of all the nations. Baptize them in the name of the
Father and of the Son and of the Holy Spirit. Teach
them to do all the things I have told you. And I am
with you always, even to the end of the world."*
MATTHEW 28:18–20

If you have accepted Jesus as your Savior, you can choose the
beautiful and brave next step of being baptized. It's a symbol
with water to represent washing away your sin and choosing
new life with Jesus. It's a way to show that you want to obey
God and be like Jesus and that you are saved from sin and
are His follower! Christians who bravely get baptized inspire
others to trust in Jesus as their Savior too.

*Dear God, help me to bravely choose baptism.
I want to show others how much I love
You and want to follow You! Amen.*

LIVE IN PEACE

When someone does something bad to you, do not pay him back with something bad. Try to do what all men know is right and good. As much as you can, live in peace with all men. Christian brothers, never pay back someone for the bad he has done to you. Let the anger of God take care of the other person. The Holy Writings say, "I will pay back to them what they should get, says the Lord."
ROMANS 12:17–19

When someone does something mean or unfair to you, you might feel like doing something mean right back to them. Everyone knows what that feeling is like. But God's Word tells us not to. It tells us not to pay back those who do bad things to us with more bad things. God wants us to let Him handle the situation. He knows exactly what happened and exactly what is fair, much better than we do. So in moments when you feel angry about an injustice done against you, choose to stop and calm down and remember that God knows and cares and wants you to live in peace while He does the hard work of making things right and fair.

☼ ☼ ☼

Dear God, please help me to live in peace even when I feel angry about the bad things others do. Help me to let You handle the situation in Your perfect way. Amen.

EXTRAORDINARY LIKE THE PROVERBS 31 WOMAN

*She is worth far more than
rubies that make one rich.*
PROVERBS 31:10

The woman described in Proverbs 31 can be a great example to you, especially these verses: "Her clothes are strength and honor. She is full of joy about the future. She opens her mouth with wisdom. The teaching of kindness is on her tongue. She looks well to the ways of those in her house, and does not eat the bread of doing nothing. Her children rise up and honor her. Her husband does also, and he praises her, saying: 'Many daughters have done well, but you have done better than all of them.' Pleasing ways lie and beauty comes to nothing, but a woman who fears the Lord will be praised" (Proverbs 31:25–30).

*Dear God, thank You for the example of the wife in Proverbs 31.
I want to do my best to live an extraordinarily good life
like she did, to be the best I can be for my family
and mostly to bring praise to You! Amen.*

SAY WHAT IS GOOD

Watch your talk! No bad words should be
coming from your mouth. Say what is good.
Your words should help others grow as Christians.
EPHESIANS 4:29

You can choose to be extraordinary in the way you talk. A lot of people use all kinds of bad or rude or ugly language these days, or they love to complain and be negative and discouraging. You can choose differently. Let the words you say be good and positive and kind. Look for ways to reach out in encouragement with your words, helping to brighten someone's day. And most of all, share the truth of God's Word with others so that they might trust Jesus as Savior and grow in their faith in Him.

🏵 🏵 🏵

Dear God, please forgive me when I don't
use my words well. Help me to watch my talk.
Please fill me up with honest, loving, and kind
words to encourage others and help them. Amen.

KEEP LOOKING TO JESUS

Let us put every thing out of our lives that keeps us from doing what we should. Let us keep running in the race that God has planned for us. Let us keep looking to Jesus. Our faith comes from Him and He is the One Who makes it perfect.
HEBREWS 12:1–2

There are so many cool things to do in life, but we sure can't do them all. It's just not possible! And there are a lot of bad things to stay away from too. The best way to live is to keep looking to Jesus, to keep reading His Word, and to keep praying and asking Him to show you the race God has mapped out specifically for you. Jesus is our example because He lived a perfect life and did exactly what God had planned for Him, and now He is sitting in the very best place in heaven forever!

Dear Jesus, I want to keep looking to You and following Your example. Please keep showing me the good race God has mapped out for me. Amen.

EXTRAORDINARY ANGELS

*"Be sure you do not hate one of these little children.
I tell you, they have angels who are always looking
into the face of My Father in heaven."*
Matthew 18:10

Maybe you hear people talk about guardian angels sometimes and wonder if they are real or not. This scripture in
the Bible tells us they are! Jesus said that little children have
angels watching over them who are also standing with God,
looking right at Him. So anything He tells them to do to help
and protect you, they know it in an instant and can come to
your rescue! Doesn't that truth make you feel brave enough
to face anything?

✿ ✿ ✿

*Dear God, thank You for the angels You have assigned
to look out for me! I'm so thankful You love and care
for me so well. Help me to be brave, knowing You
always help and protect and rescue me! Amen.*

GROWING STRONG AND HEALTHY

*Keep yourself growing in God-like living. Growing strong
in body is all right but growing in God-like living is more
important. It will not only help you in this life now but in the
next life also. These words are true and they can be trusted.
Because of this, we work hard and do our best because
our hope is in the living God, the One Who would save
all men. He saves those who believe in Him.*
1 TIMOTHY 4:7–10

There are a bazillion popular ways to keep your body strong
and in shape these days. And that's good. The Bible tells us we
definitely should take good care of our bodies (see 1 Corinthians 6:19–20). But even more important, the Bible tells us we
should grow in God-like living. We should love to learn more
and more about God and to live like His Son, Jesus. Growing
strong in our bodies here on earth matters for a little while,
but growing strong in knowing and loving God matters for
forever.

*Dear God, help me to grow strong and healthy in my body,
and even more importantly, help me to keep growing stronger
and healthier in living for You and obeying You! Amen.*

THE WOMAN WHO NEEDED HEALING

*A woman had been sick for twelve years with a flow of blood.
(*She had spent all the money she had on doctors.) But she
could not be healed by anyone. She came behind Jesus and
touched the bottom of His coat. At once the flow of blood
stopped. Jesus said, "Who touched Me?" Everyone said that
they had not touched Him. Peter said, "Teacher, so many people
are pushing You from every side and You say, 'Who touched
Me?' " Then Jesus said, "Someone touched Me because I know
power has gone from Me." When the woman saw she could not
hide it, she came shaking. She got down before Jesus. Then she
told Jesus in front of all the people why she had touched Him.
She told how she was healed at once. Jesus said to her,
"Daughter, your faith has healed you. Go in peace."*

LUKE 8:43–48

If you've ever had a sickness that dragged on and on, you
know how sick of being sick you get, even for a matter of days
or weeks. The poor bleeding woman in the Bible had been
sick for twelve years! But she had heard of Jesus, and she
had great faith in His power. She was sure that if she just
touched the bottom of His coat, she would be healed. So she
did, and she was!

*Dear God, help me to have extraordinary faith
like the woman who needed Your healing. Amen.*

ABOVE AND BEYOND

*I pray that Christ may live in your hearts by faith. I pray
that you will be filled with love. I pray that you will be able
to understand how wide and how long and how high and how
deep His love is. I pray that you will know the love of Christ.
His love goes beyond anything we can understand. I pray that
you will be filled with God Himself. God is able to do much
more than we ask or think through His power working in us.*
EPHESIANS 3:17–20

God's love to us through Jesus is above and beyond anything
we can imagine, and so is His power working in us. When we
focus on that truth instead of our worries and fears, we can
have extraordinary courage to do anything God asks us to.

*Dear God, I choose to focus on Your incredible
love and power in my life. Please fill me and
do Your good work through me. Amen.*

96

CONFESSION

*If we say that we have no sin, we lie to ourselves and
the truth is not in us. If we tell Him our sins, He is
faithful and we can depend on Him to forgive us of
our sins. He will make our lives clean from all sin.*
1 JOHN 1:8–9

It's not fun to talk about the sinful things we've done wrong,
but we need to tell them to God. To pretend like we don't
sin sometimes is silly because God knows anyway. He sees
and knows everything about us, even every single thought we
have. So take time to pray and confess and ask forgiveness
for your sins rather than try to hide them or act like they're
no big deal. As soon as we do confess our sins, God cleans us
up and takes the sin as far from us as the east is from the west
(see Psalm 103:12). Amazing! He loves us so much and never
wants to hold our sins against us.

*Dear God, I confess these sins to you today: _____ ;
I ask for Your forgiveness. Thank You for being such a good and
forgiving God who gives me endless grace and love! Amen.*

EXTRAORDINARY GUIDE

*The Lord went before them, in a pillar of cloud during
the day to lead them on the way, and in a pillar of fire
during the night to give them light. So they could travel
day and night. The pillar of cloud during the day and the
pillar of fire during the night did not leave the people.*
EXODUS 13:21–22

God is the best guide! When He led His people, the Israelites,
out of slavery in Egypt, He did so in a pillar of cloud during the
day and a pillar of fire at night to give them light. That must
have been an incredible sight! When you read this story in the
Bible, let it remind you that God can lead you in extraordinary
ways too. Ask Him to do so and to help you know when and
where He is leading!

✿ ✿ ✿

*Dear God, I trust that You can use anything to
lead me in my life. Please keep my ears and eyes
and mind open and wise to hear and see and
know all the ways You want to guide me. Amen.*

THE GREATEST COMMANDMENTS

"Teacher, which one is the greatest of the Laws?" Jesus said to him, "'You must love the Lord your God with all your heart and with all your soul and with all your mind.' This is the first and greatest of the Laws. The second is like it, 'You must love your neighbor as you love yourself.' All the Laws and the writings of the early preachers depend on these two most important Laws."
MATTHEW 22:36–40

Jesus said the most important commandments to obey are to love God first with all your heart, soul, and mind and to love your neighbor as yourself. If you do these things first in your life, you will automatically do other things well too. Because as you love God with all your heart, soul, and mind, you will be wanting to learn more and more about Him. And as you constantly learn about Him and grow closer to Him plus love others as you love yourself, you'll find yourself living the life He has planned for you—the most extraordinary and best!

❀ ❀ ❀

Dear God, I do want to love You with all my heart, soul, and mind, and I want to love others as I love myself. Please always help me to put these two things first in my life. Amen.

EXTRAORDINARY LIKE HANNAH: PART 1

*[Hannah] gave him the name Samuel,
saying, "I have asked the Lord for him."*
1 SAMUEL 1:20

A woman named Hannah in the Bible desperately wanted to be a mother, but she had no children. She cried and prayed, asking God to let her have a baby boy. Sometimes she felt like God had forgotten about her or didn't care about her. But still Hannah kept praying. She made an extraordinary promise to God, saying, "If You give me a son, I will give him back to You for all the days of his life."

A religious leader named Eli had watched Hannah praying. After talking with her, he said, "Go peacefully, and may the God of Israel give you what you have asked."

Right away, Hannah felt much better. She went home with her husband and soon she did have a baby boy! She named him Samuel, saying, "I asked the Lord for him" (see 1 Samuel 1:10–20).

☙ ❀ ☙

*Dear God, even if I'm feeling forgotten by You,
like Hannah did for a while, help me to keep
on praying and trusting You! Amen.*

EXTRAORDINARY LIKE HANNAH: PART 2

*Hannah prayed and said, "My heart is happy
in the Lord. My strength is honored in the
Lord. . . . There is no one holy like the Lord."*
1 Samuel 2:1–2

Hannah loved and cared for baby Samuel, but she never forgot her prayers and her promise to God. When the little boy was old enough, Hannah returned to Shiloh to the tabernacle where she had met Eli. She said, "I asked for my son, and God gave him to me. So now I give him back to God for his whole life." Hannah meant she was letting Samuel live at the tabernacle to grow up and be a servant of God there under the care of Eli.

Every year Hannah came back to the tabernacle to visit Samuel. And God blessed Hannah with three more sons and two daughters. She was greatly rewarded for being faithful to the Lord.

Samuel grew to be a very important leader and speaker for God. He was a blessing to all the people of Israel because Hannah kept her promise to God about her son.

✿ ✿ ✿

*Dear God, help me to be brave like Hannah
and always keep my promises to You! Amen.*

POWERFUL LOVE

Nothing can keep us from the love of God. Death cannot!
Life cannot! Angels cannot! Leaders cannot! Any other
power cannot! Hard things now or in the future cannot!
The world above or the world below cannot! Any other
living thing cannot keep us away from the love of God
which is ours through Christ Jesus our Lord.
ROMANS 8:38–39

There are days when you might feel unloved and maybe
scared that you will never be loved again. You will need to
remember these verses from Romans 8—God's love for you
is unlike any other kind of love, and absolutely nothing can
ever stop it. God shares it with you in all kinds of ways and
through many different people. Ask Him to show you His
extraordinary love every day, and then thank and praise Him
as He gives it.

❀ ❀ ❀

Dear God, please remind me that I am never unloved.
You love me more powerfully than I can possibly
imagine, and I love You too! Amen.

EXTRAORDINARY LIKE MARY, JOANNA, AND SUSANNA

*After this Jesus went to all the cities and towns preaching
and telling the Good News about the holy nation of God.
The twelve followers were with Him. Some women who
had been healed of demons and diseases were with Him.
Mary Magdalene, who had had seven demons put out of her,
was one of them. Joanna, the wife of Chuza who was one
of Herod's helpers, was another one. Susanna and many
others also cared for Jesus by using what they had.*

LUKE 8:1–3

Mary Magdalene, Joanna, and Susanna are three women
mentioned in the Bible who were healed by Jesus from demons and diseases. Then they traveled around with Jesus as
He went to many cities and towns to share the good news.
What a great way to show how thankful they were! Jesus
helped them and then they traveled with Him to help Him
spread the amazing news of God's love!

✿ ✿ ✿

*Dear Jesus, You have helped me so much, and I am so
thankful! I want to share how You have helped me so
that others will want to know You as Savior too! Amen.*

STRONG HEART

Good will come to the man who is ready to give much, and fair in what he does. He will never be shaken. The man who is right and good will be remembered forever. He will not be afraid of bad news. His heart is strong because he trusts in the Lord.
PSALM 112:5–7

The way this is written in the Bible makes it sound like it's a promise just for a man, but the promise is for you too! Good will come to you when you are generous and fair. You will not be shaken. You don't need to be afraid of bad news. Your heart is strong because you trust in God. When you live your life focusing on this kind of truth from God's Word, you gain extraordinary courage to live your days not worrying or living in fear but doing what God has planned for you!

Dear God, thank You for the promises in Your Word for me! I trust in You and I'm so grateful You make my heart strong! Amen.

EXTRAORDINARY WORK ETHIC

*Do not be lazy but always work hard. Work for
the Lord with a heart full of love for Him.*
ROMANS 12:11

Do you know what it means to have a good work ethic? It means to be willing to work hard and do your best with the gifts and talents God has given you. It doesn't mean you should never take a break or a rest or just have some fun. Of course you need all that too! And as a kid your playtime is often your work as you're learning and growing through being creative and active. But it's easy in this world to take too many breaks and have too much rest and too much fun. When you have schoolwork to do, do your very best at it. When you have chores to do and things to take care of, work hard and be cheerful and loving. Think of God as the boss overseeing you, because He ultimately is, but He's the best kind of boss—full of love and blessing for you as you do the good work He gives you.

*Dear God, please give me a work ethic that shows
others I work to please You most of all. Please help
me to find lots of joy in my work. You are so good,
and it is an honor to do my best for You! Amen.*

NO ONE LIKE GOD

Then King David went in and sat before the Lord, and said, "Who am I, O Lord God, and what is my family, that You have brought me this far? Yet this was a small thing in Your eyes, O Lord God. You have spoken of Your servant's family in the future. And this is the way of man, O Lord God. What more can David say to You? For You know Your servant, O Lord God. Because of Your Word and Your own heart, You have done all these great things to let Your servant know. For this reason You are great, O Lord God. There is none like You. And there is no God but You, by all that we have heard with our ears."
2 Samuel 7:18–22

Like King David did, we should pray to God and focus on His greatness and all He does for us. The one, true, all-powerful God of the whole universe knows you and loves you and takes care of you! Wow! No one else is like God. He is the most extraordinary of all, and He is with you and for you. Call to Him in anything and everything and let Him guide you and help you.

🌼 🌼 🌼

Dear God, I praise You and thank You for who You are and Your extraordinary power and love for me. Amen.

EXTRAORDINARY FAITH

*Jesus came to the city of Capernaum. A captain of
the army came to Him. He asked for help, saying, "Lord,
my servant is sick in bed. He is not able to move his body.
He is in much pain." Jesus said to the captain, "I will come
and heal him." The captain said, "Lord, I am not good enough
for You to come to my house. Only speak the word, and my
servant will be healed. I am a man who works for someone
else and I have men working under me. I say to this man,
'Go!' and he goes. I say to another, 'Come!' and he comes.
I say to my servant, 'Do this!' and he does it."*

MATTHEW 8:5–9

This army captain had such extraordinary faith in Jesus, he
didn't even ask Jesus to come back to his house to heal his
servant. He trusted Jesus could just say the word from anywhere and his servant would be healed. And the captain was
absolutely right! Jesus said to him, " 'Go your way. It is done
for you even as you had faith to believe.' The servant was
healed at that time" (Matthew 8:13).

*Dear God, I want to have extraordinary faith like this
army captain. Help me to trust that You can simply say
the word and absolutely anything can happen! Amen.*

EXTRAORDINARY FAMILY

Teach these things so they will do what is right.
Anyone who does not take care of his family and
those in his house has turned away from the faith. He is
worse than a person who has never put his trust in Christ.
1 TIMOTHY 5:7–8

Family matters to God and should matter to you too! God has placed you in the family you have, and it's important to get along well and take care of each other. Of course you will get upset and annoyed with each other sometimes, but with God's help you can work things out with forgiveness and grace and love for each other. Remember this scripture to help you: "Try to understand other people. Forgive each other. If you have something against someone, forgive him. That is the way the Lord forgave you. And to all these things, you must add love" (Colossians 3:13–14).

Dear God, thank You for my family. Please help
us to love each other and take care of each
other like You want us to. Amen.

DON'T GET TRAPPED

A God-like life gives us much when we are happy for what we have. We came into this world with nothing. For sure, when we die, we will take nothing with us. If we have food and clothing, let us be happy. But men who want lots of money are tempted. They are trapped into doing all kinds of foolish things and things which hurt them. These things drag them into sin and will destroy them. The love of money is the beginning of all kinds of sin. Some people have turned from the faith because of their love for money. They have made much pain for themselves because of this.

1 Timothy 6:6–10

A lot of people base their goals in life on what will help them gain more money. Choose now while you are young not to make money the focus of your goals. Instead, trust God's Word that getting trapped in wanting lots of money can lead to all kinds of sin and foolish things. Let Him help you focus on goals that match up with His good plans for your life.

Dear God, I don't want my goals to be about money; I want them to be about serving You! Please help me keep my focus on all the best things You have planned for me. Amen.

EXTRAORDINARY LIKE MARY, THE MOTHER OF JESUS

*Mary said, "My heart sings with thanks for my Lord.
And my spirit is happy in God, the One Who saves from
the punishment of sin. The Lord has looked on me, His
servant-girl and one who is not important. But from now
on all people will honor me. He Who is powerful has done
great things for me. His name is holy. The loving-kindness of
the Lord is given to the people of all times who honor Him."*

LUKE 1:46–50

You know from all the Christmastime stories that the mother
of baby Jesus was named Mary. To be the mother of the
Savior of the world is truly extraordinary! Especially when it
all came as a total shock and through a miracle of the Holy
Spirit. Mary must have been scared at first, but in response
to the angel from God who told her the news, she said, "I am
willing to be used of the Lord. Let it happen to me as you have
said" (Luke 1:38). And later she praised God with the scripture
we read in Luke 1:46–55, which is often called Mary's Song or
in Latin the *Magnificat*.

✿ ✿ ✿

*Dear God, no matter what You ask me to do in life,
and no matter how hard it might be, I want to have
the kind of response Mary did. I want to be willing to do
anything for You and praise You through all of it. I know
You are good and You only ask good things of me. Amen.*

LET GOD REFRESH YOU

*The Lord will always lead you. He will meet the needs
of your soul in the dry times and give strength to
your body. You will be like a garden that has enough
water, like a well of water that never dries up.*

Isaiah 58:11

Do you have plants in your home that are near death because no one remembers to water them? They start to look really sad, don't they? Or think of your lawn or garden in the middle of a hot summer with no rain. It's brown and kinda crispy, right? Sometimes we start to feel dry and ugly like that in our souls when we aren't spending good time with God. We need to read His Word and pray and worship Him so that He can lead and refresh us. He can give us living water so that we never feel thirsty again!

*Dear God, thank You for refreshing me with
Your extraordinary living water! Amen.*

EXTRAORDINARY RESPONSE

*If men speak bad of you because you are a Christian, you will
be happy because the Spirit of shining-greatness and of God
is in you. . . . But if a man suffers as a Christian, he should not
be ashamed. He should thank God that he is a Christian.*
1 PETER 4:14, 16

If you are ever ridiculed for being a Christian, you can respond
in an extraordinary way—be happy about it! That's not always
easy, but God's Word tells us we should not be ashamed.
We should be thankful! God's Spirit is in us and we are saved
forever, so we don't need to worry about what anyone else
might say to tease us or be mean to us. Matthew 5:11–12 (NLT)
says, "God blesses you when people mock you and persecute
you and lie about you and say all sorts of evil things against
you because you are my followers. Be happy about it! Be very
glad! For a great reward awaits you in heaven."

*Dear Jesus, help me not to get angry if people
tease me or act mean because I love and follow You.
Remind me to be happy because You have saved me
and have a great reward for me in heaven. Amen.*

THE VINE AND THE BRANCHES

"I am the true Vine. My Father is the One Who cares for the Vine. He takes away any branch in Me that does not give fruit. Any branch that gives fruit, He cuts it back so it will give more fruit. You are made clean by the words I have spoken to you. Get your life from Me and I will live in you. No branch can give fruit by itself. It has to get life from the vine. You are able to give fruit only when you have life from Me. I am the Vine and you are the branches. Get your life from Me. Then I will live in you and you will give much fruit."

JOHN 15:1–5

Jesus described Himself as like a vine and God the Father as like the gardener. We are the branches. The fruit that we grow on our branches are the good things we do for God that He has planned for us—like serving and giving to others, sharing God's love, and helping others know Jesus as Savior. And we can't produce any good fruit unless we stay connected to Jesus the Vine!

Dear Jesus, I want my life to come only from You. Help me to stay connected to You and grow the good fruit You want me to. Amen.

EXTRAORDINARY LIKE ELIZABETH

There was a Jewish religious leader named Zacharias. . . . His wife was of the family group of Aaron. Her name was Elizabeth. They were right with God and obeyed the Jewish Law and did what the Lord said to do. They had no children because Elizabeth was not able to have a child. Both of them were older people.

LUKE 1:5–7

Elizabeth and her husband, Zacharias, both thought they were far too old to have children, but God sent the angel Gabriel to tell Zacharias that Elizabeth would have a special baby and they should name him John. Zacharias did not believe Gabriel's message, and because of his unbelief God made him unable to speak. But soon "Elizabeth knew she was to become a mother. . . . She said, 'This is what the Lord has done for me' " (Luke 1:24–25).

Then, "when the time came, Elizabeth gave birth to a son. Her neighbors and family heard how the Lord had shown loving-kindness to her. They were happy for her. . . . They named him Zacharias, after his father. But his mother said, 'No! His name is John' " (Luke 1:57–60). Zacharias agreed, and then he was able to talk again. John grew to be an important preacher and teacher, preparing the way for people to believe in Jesus.

*Dear God, Elizabeth believed in and obeyed You,
even when things seemed impossible! I want
to believe and obey that way too. Amen.*

OUR STRENGTH AND STRONG PLACE

*I will sing of Your strength. Yes, I will sing with joy of Your
loving-kindness in the morning. For You have been a strong
and safe place for me in times of trouble. O my Strength,
I will sing praises to You. For God is my strong place
and the God Who shows me loving-kindness.*
PSALM 59:16–17

As you're growing up, your strength grows a little every day,
especially if you're in sports or other activities that use your
muscles a lot. But nothing compares to God as your ultimate
source of strength. His extraordinary strength is far beyond
any kind of human strength. When you choose to focus on
it and even sing about it in praise to God, you are filled with
courage. You remember you don't ever need to depend on
your own strength when you have God with you.

*Dear God, You are my Strength, and I love You and praise
You. I know You are strong enough to do anything to
help and protect me whenever I need it. Amen.*

SADNESS INTO JOY

*Hear, O Lord. And show me loving-kindness. O Lord,
be my Helper. You have turned my crying into dancing.*
PSALM 30:10–11

Only our extraordinary God can take the worst kind of sadness or anger or pain in our lives and turn it into such joy we feel like dancing. He might do that for us here on earth in certain ways, or we might have to wait until heaven, but He promises that He will. With every hard thing you might go through, you have a choice either to let your circumstances make you angry and pull you apart from God or to trust His promise and grow closer to Him. The first choice will only make you sadder and sadder, but the second choice will make you end up happy dancing!

*Dear God, please help me want to get closer and closer
to You when I am sad or angry or upset. I trust that
You will turn it all into total joy someday. Amen.*

STRAIGHT PATHS

Trust in the Lord with all your heart, and do not trust in your own understanding. Agree with Him in all your ways, and He will make your paths straight. Do not be wise in your own eyes. Fear the Lord and turn away from what is sinful.
PROVERBS 3:5–7

Even though so many movies and stories and people today will tell you to trust your heart and follow your dreams, that's not always the best advice. Before you do, make sure your heart and your dreams match up with God's. Too often our own hearts and dreams are tempted by what is sinful and bad for us. So His Word tells us to trust Him with all our hearts and not to lean on our own understanding. We need to stay close to Him through reading His Word, praying, worshipping Him, and serving Him, and we constantly have to ask Him to help us agree with Him in our ways. We can trust Him to make straight paths for our dreams when they match up with His perfect plans for our lives.

Dear God, I want to trust in You more than myself. Please match my dreams to Yours for me and make my paths straight. Amen.

EXTRAORDINARY LIKE LYDIA

*On the Day of Rest we went outside the city to a place
down by the river. We thought people would be gathering
there for prayer. Some women came and we sat down
and talked to them. One of the women who listened sold
purple cloth. She was from the city of Thyatira. Her name
was Lydia and she was a worshiper of God. The Lord
opened her heart to hear what Paul said.*

ACTS 16:13–14

A woman named Lydia in the Bible had a business selling
purple cloth, and because that was the color of royalty, she
probably made a lot of money. Sometimes people with a lot
of money think they don't need anything else in their lives
except money. They think they can buy any kind of happiness
and peace. But Lydia worshipped God and wanted to listen
to what the followers of Jesus had to say. And the Bible says
the Lord "opened her heart" and she accepted Jesus as her
Savior. He alone gives true happiness and peace and ever-
lasting life!

✿ ✿ ✿

*Dear God, no matter what good things or how much money
I am blessed with in this life, I still need You and salvation
through Jesus. Thank You for Lydia's example to me. Amen.*

EXTRAORDINARY GIFTS

*God has given each of you a gift. Use it to help each other.
This will show God's loving-favor. If a man preaches, let him
do it with God speaking through him. If a man helps others,
let him do it with the strength God gives. So in all things God
may be honored through Jesus Christ. Shining-greatness
and power belong to Him forever. Let it be so.*
1 PETER 4:10–11

The talents and things you are naturally good at and that
come easy to you are the gifts God has given you. He has
given them to you so you can help others with them. If you're
good at math, see what you can do to help your friends who
struggle with it. If you're especially good at being friendly
and outgoing, reach out to the new kids at school. If you have
talents in music, see how you can use them to help worship
God at church. Most of all, constantly thank God and give
credit to Him for every cool thing you can do. Each one is a
gift from Him!

*Dear God, thank You for the awesome talents and
abilities You have given me. I want to use all of them
to worship You and tell others about You! Amen.*

BECAUSE YOU HAVE FAITH

Jesus went on from there. Two blind men followed Him. They called out, "Take pity on us, Son of David." Jesus went into the house. The blind men came to Him. Then Jesus said to them, "Do you have faith that I can do this?" They said to Him, "Yes, Sir!" Then Jesus put His hands on their eyes and said, "You will have what you want because you have faith." Their eyes were opened.
MATTHEW 9:27–30

You don't usually ask someone to do something for you and then say something like "You probably won't do it, though." That's kind of silly, isn't it? So don't pray that way either! When you ask God for something in prayer, tell Him what you need and then remember He is absolutely able to do it. Tell Him you know He is able to do it. Then tell Him you have faith in Him to answer and you trust His will.

Dear Jesus, I have faith You can do anything! Nothing I ask of You is too hard for You. You are amazing! Amen.

AN EXTRAORDINARY LUNCH

*"There is a boy here who has five loaves of barley bread
and two small fish. What is that for so many people?"
Jesus said, "Have the people sit down." There was much
grass in that place. About five thousand men sat down.*

JOHN 6:9–10

Maybe your school lunches are usually ham sandwiches and
carrot sticks or your favorite cafeteria pizza. In Bible times,
there was a young boy who brought five loaves of bread and
two small fish for his lunch when he went to hear Jesus teach.
But soon Jesus took those loaves and fish and turned them
into enough food to feed all five thousand hungry men who
were there, plus many more women and children—and there
were twelve baskets of leftovers! Can you imagine if you and
your school lunch were part of that extraordinary miracle?
Let this true story remind you of how awesome Jesus is and
how He can provide for all people in any way He chooses.

🌸 🌸 🌸

*Dear Jesus, You are so amazing to be able to do any
miracle at all! I don't ever want to forget how You
provide for Your people in extraordinary ways. Amen.*

DON'T GIVE UP

I did not give up waiting for the Lord. And He turned to me and heard my cry. He brought me up out of the hole of danger, out of the mud and clay. He set my feet on a rock, making my feet sure. He put a new song in my mouth, a song of praise to our God. Many will see and fear and will put their trust in the Lord.
PSALM 40:1–3

Even when it seems like God is taking forever to answer your prayers, don't give up. Keep waiting for Him! At just the right time, He will answer and help you according to His will. And like this psalm says, He will bring you out of danger and onto solid rock. Then you'll be singing new songs to God, and many will see what happened and hear your praise and put their trust in God too!

Dear God, I never want to give up waiting for You. Please help me to keep hanging on for just the right time that You have planned. Amen.

EXTRAORDINARY LIKE JAIRUS'S DAUGHTER

Jairus was one of the leaders of the Jewish place of worship. As Jairus came to Jesus, he got down at His feet. He cried out to Jesus and said, "My little daughter is almost dead. Come and put Your hand on her that she may be healed and live." Jesus went with him.
MARK 5:22–24

Jairus's daughter was only twelve years old. We don't know what illness she had that made her so sick, but we know that she was dearly loved by her dad and mom and many others. Her dad had great faith that Jesus could come and simply put His hand on her and she would live. And Jairus was right. Jesus told him not to be afraid but to believe, and then He went home with Jairus to the room were his daughter lay. Jesus told the many people crying for her that she was only sleeping, but they laughed at Him. Then Jesus told everyone except Jairus and his wife to leave the room. He took their daughter by the hand and said, "Little girl, I say to you, get up!" (Mark 5:41). Right away, she got up, good as new!

☘ ☘ ☘

Dear God, You are the amazing God of life and miracles! Thank You for the awesome ways Jesus showed us Your love and Your power to heal and give life. Amen.

THE ONE WHO MAKES THE MOUNTAINS

He is the One Who makes the mountains and the wind.
He makes His thoughts known to man. He turns the
morning into darkness, and walks on the high places
of the earth. The Lord God of All is His name.

AMOS 4:13

Have you ever spent time in the mountains? Then you know how high and strong they are. Can you imagine God easily walking around on top of them? That's incredible to think about, and the Bible says He can! When you are facing problems or fears that seem like mountains that are way too tall for you to ever get over, picture the Lord God of all walking on top of them and then reaching down His hand to help you over them.

❀ ❀ ❀

Dear God, I believe You are able to help me
overcome any problems that seem like unmoving
mountains in my life. Please keep holding my
hand and helping me over them. Amen.

STEP AWAY AND STAY AWAY

Do not want to be like those who do wrong. . . .
Trust in the Lord, and do good. So you will live in
the land and will be fed. Be happy in the Lord.
And He will give you the desires of your heart.
PSALM 37:1–4

It's not always easy to stay away from those who do wrong. Sometimes it seems fun to just go along with whatever seems popular, even if deep down you know what is popular is wrong. So it takes courage to step away from those doing wrong, especially if you're feeling pressure from people you thought were your friends. But God promises if you trust Him and do good, you will have everything you need and He will give you the things that make you happy because first you are happy in Him!

✿ ✿ ✿

Dear God, please help me to have courage to step away
and stay away from those who do wrong. I want to do
the good and right things that make You happy. I trust
that's the best way for me to be happy too. Amen.

THE ONE WHO SAVES

First of all, I ask you to pray much for all men and to give thanks for them. Pray for kings and all others who are in power over us so we might live quiet God-like lives in peace. It is good when you pray like this. It pleases God Who is the One Who saves. He wants all people to be saved from the punishment of sin. He wants them to come to know the truth. There is one God. There is one Man standing between God and men. That Man is Christ Jesus. He gave His life for all men so they could go free and not be held by the power of sin.
1 TIMOTHY 2:1–6

Our God is an extraordinary Savior. He sent Jesus to give His life so that all people could be totally free from the power of sin and the death it leads to. He wants everyone to believe in the truth about Jesus. Those who trust in Jesus as their Savior from sin never really die, because forever perfect life is waiting for us in heaven.

✿ ✿ ✿

Dear God, thank You for being an extraordinary Savior who wants all people to believe in the truth of Jesus. I pray for those people who do not yet believe, and I am so grateful that I do believe in You! Amen.

BE AN EXTRAORDINARY GIVER

*Tell those who are rich in this world not to be proud and
not to trust in their money. Money cannot be trusted.
They should put their trust in God. He gives us all we need
for our happiness. Tell them to do good and be rich in good
works. They should give much to those in need and be ready
to share. Then they will be gathering together riches for
themselves. These good things are what they will build on
for the future. Then they will have the only true life!*

1 TIMOTHY 6:17–19

As you dream about what your job might be when you grow
up and how much money you might make, start thinking now
while you are young about how to be a generous giver with
your money and with your blessings. God's Word tells us all
to be ready to share and give and help others in need—and
promises that we will gather up forever treasure in heaven by
doing so. Money and treasures of this world will not last forever; only the good and giving kinds of things we have done
here on earth will matter in heaven.

*Dear God, help me to start thinking even now
about how I can be an extraordinary giver. Amen.*

REMEMBER WHEN

Moses said to the people, "Remember this day in which you went out of Egypt, out of the land where you were made to stay and work. For the Lord brought you out of this place by a powerful hand."
EXODUS 13:3

Sometimes we just want to forget the bad things that have happened to us because they were awful and we're so glad they're over. But to an extent we do need to remember them so that we never forget how God helped us through them and rescued us from them. Looking back and remembering grows our faith and helps us trust that God will always help and rescue again in the future. Moses told the people of Israel to remember the amazing day that God finally brought them out of slavery in Egypt. Just like they did, we also need to remember all the incredible ways God has helped us and rescued us from trouble.

Dear God, every bit of help and rescue I have ever received ultimately came from You! I don't ever want to forget, and I trust You to help and rescue me again and again. I am so grateful for Your faithfulness! Amen.

EXTRAORDINARY ENDURANCE

We are pressed on every side, but we still have room to move. We are often in much trouble, but we never give up. People make it hard for us, but we are not left alone. We are knocked down, but we are not destroyed.

2 CORINTHIANS 4:8–9

Endurance means to not give up but to keep on going even when things are hard. Maybe you've shown great endurance during a sport or activity like cross-country or dance. Or maybe you've shown great endurance during a really hard test at school when you felt super stressed and wanted to give up, but you didn't. God's Word describes how sometimes we will have so much trouble we'll feel like we are almost totally defeated. But God will always help us have just enough new strength and energy and endurance so we can choose not to give up.

Dear God, You keep giving me more and more strength and energy and endurance exactly when I need it. I never have to give up when I know You are helping me! Amen.

WHEN THE SUN AND MOON STOOD STILL

Then Joshua spoke to the Lord on the day when the Lord made the Amorites lose the war against the sons of Israel. He said, in the eyes of Israel, "O sun, stand still at Gibeon. O moon, stand still in the valley of Aijalon." So the sun stood still and the moon stopped, until the nation punished those who fought against them. Is it not written in the Book of Jashar? The sun stopped in the center of the sky. It did not hurry to go down for about a whole day. There has been no day like it before or since, when the Lord listened to the voice of a man. For the Lord fought for Israel.

JOSHUA 10:12–14

This was an extraordinary miracle, for sure—a day when God stopped the sun and moon in the sky to help His people defeat their enemies. Remember that if God is able to do that for His people, He is able to do anything for you as well. Keep calling on Him for His help with anything you need.

Dear God, help me remember Your extraordinary ways and Your ability to help me with anything. Amen.

EXTRAORDINARY CARE

*The next day Jesus went to a city called Nain. His followers
and many other people went with Him. When they came
near the city gate, a dead man was being carried out. He
was the only son of a woman whose husband had died. Many
people of the city were with her. When the Lord saw her, He
had loving-pity for her and said, "Do not cry." He went and put
His hand on the box in which the dead man was carried. The
men who were carrying it, stopped. Jesus said, "Young man,
I say to you, get up!" The man who was dead sat up and
began to talk. Then Jesus gave him to his mother.*

LUKE 7:11–15

In Bible times, if a woman had no husband and no sons, she
was in a dangerous situation. It was very hard for a woman to
provide for herself and protect herself without a man back
then. So when Jesus saw this widow whose son had just died,
He had extra concern for her and told her not to cry. Then
Jesus brought her dead son back to life and gave him back to
his mother. Can you imagine how happy she must have been?

*Dear Jesus, thank You for Your miracles! Your concern
and love for others are truly extraordinary. You care
so much about people who are in awful situations.
Help me to care like You do. Amen.*

EXTRAORDINARY LIGHT

*God is helping you obey Him. God is doing what He wants done
in you. Be glad you can do the things you should be doing. Do
all things without arguing and talking about how you wish you
did not have to do them. In that way, you can prove yourselves
to be without blame. You are God's children and no one can
talk against you, even in a sin-loving and sin-sick world. You are
to shine as lights among the sinful people of this world.*
PHILIPPIANS 2:13–15

It's sure hard to do all things without ever arguing or complaining, isn't it? But that's what this scripture encourages us
to do. It's something we all need a lot of help from God with.
But if we can stay positive as we obey God and follow the
plans He has for us, we shine as extrabright lights to the sinful
world around us. And hopefully people who don't yet trust
Jesus as their Savior will want to know more about God's love
because they see our lights shining.

*Dear God, please help me to be extraordinary light in the
darkness of sin around me in this world. I want to shine so
brightly so that others might know Jesus as Savior too. Amen.*

WATCHING OVER YOU

*For You are my hope, O Lord God. You are my trust
since I was young. You have kept me safe from birth.
It was You Who watched over me from the day
I was born. My praise is always of You.*

PSALM 71:5–6

You have a lot of people in your life who take care of you—parents, grandparents, aunts and uncles and other relatives, friends, teachers, school staff, coaches, doctors, nurses, and on and on. But God is the One who constantly watches over you. Praise and thank Him for His extraordinary care. He is the One working through all of those who take care of you and teach you good things in your life. And He will keep watching over you all your life, like Psalm 23:6 says: "For sure, You will give me goodness and loving-kindness all the days of my life. Then I will live with You in Your house forever."

*Dear God, thank You so much for watching
over me and guiding me through so many
different people in my life. Amen.*

EXTRAORDINARY COMFORT

We give thanks to the God and Father of our Lord Jesus Christ. He is our Father Who shows us loving-kindness and our God Who gives us comfort. He gives us comfort in all our troubles. Then we can comfort other people who have the same troubles. We give the same kind of comfort God gives us.

2 Corinthians 1:3–4

You might like all kinds of things that give you comfort, like your favorite foods, your coziest blanket, your comfiest sweatshirt, and the best spot on the couch. Pets and stuffed animals can give so much comfort too. And of course the comfort that comes from a loving hug or hand from a parent or grandparent or good friend is one of the best kinds of all! When you are lovingly comforted in any good way, that comfort is coming from God. He knows every time you need extra comfort and love and He gives it in many ways through many people. Then when you feel better you can share the kinds of comfort you received with others. It's a beautiful cycle that God designed!

Dear God, thank You for every bit of comfort I get exactly when I need it, and please help me to share comfort exactly when others need it too! Amen.

ABSOLUTELY ANYTHING

Then Moses put out his hand over the sea. And the Lord moved the sea all night by a strong east wind. So the waters were divided. And the people of Israel went through the sea on dry land. The waters were like a wall to them on their right and on their left.

EXODUS 14:21–22

Do you know the story of God parting the Red Sea for Moses and the Israelites to bring them safely out of Egypt? It's so cool to stop and think about how amazing that must have been. Next time you're at the lake or the beach, just imagine if all the waters suddenly moved and made a pathway for you to walk through. That sounds crazy, right? But that's how crazy awesome our one, true, extraordinary God is. Anytime you're near a body of water, think about how He is able to do absolutely anything to help you in your life.

Dear God, You are so cool and so powerful.
I trust that You can do absolutely anything! Amen.

EXTRAORDINARY LIKE THE WOMAN AT THE WELL

A woman of Samaria came to get water.
JOHN 4:7

One day on His travels, Jesus sat down near a well. When a Samaritan woman came to get water from the well, Jesus asked her, "Could you please give Me a drink?"

Usually Jewish people had nothing to do with Samaritan people. So the woman asked Jesus, "Why are You asking me for a drink?"

But it didn't matter to Jesus that the woman was a Samaritan. He loved every person, no matter what country they were from. He said to her, "If you only knew how wonderful the gift is that God wants to give to you, you would actually be the one asking *Me* for water. And then I would give you living water."

The woman didn't understand. She said to Jesus, "Where will You get this water? This well is deep, and You don't have any kind of jug with You for fetching water."

Jesus said to her, "Whoever drinks the water from this well will be thirsty again. But whoever drinks the water that I give will never be thirsty. The water that I give to people becomes a well of life inside that lasts forever."

The woman said, "Sir, please give me this water so I will never be thirsty" (see John 4:7–15).

❀ ❀ ❀

Dear Jesus, please help me to believe You like the woman at the well did. She trusted that You give the kind of water that makes people never thirst again, and I trust You too! Amen.

136

EXTRAORDINARY POWER

I pray that you will see how great the things are that He has promised to those who belong to Him. I pray that you will know how great His power is for those who have put their trust in Him. It is the same power that raised Christ from the dead.

EPHESIANS 1:18–20

Paul in the Bible was writing a letter to the Christians who lived in Ephesus, and he was sharing his prayers for them. Those same prayers are what God wants for you as a Christian today too. If you believe in Jesus as your only Savior, you belong to Him and you have hope for the awesome things God has planned for you. And His power for you is so great—it is the same power that brought Jesus back to life! That extraordinary power is working in you now so you can do the good things God wants for you, and it will be working in you forever, because it has given you eternal life.

Dear God, help me to see and know more and more every day how awesome You are and how awesome Your plans and Your power in my life are. Amen.

SOLID ROCK

The Lord is my rock, and my safe place, and the One Who takes me out of trouble. My God is my rock, in Whom I am safe. He is my safe-covering, my saving strength, and my strong tower.
PSALM 18:2

If you've ever crossed a rope bridge, you know how shaky it feels. It's fun at a playground, but what if it were the only way to try to cross to safety over a wild river in a dangerous jungle? Then you might not think it's so fun, right? You'd probably be wishing for something rock solid. Anytime something in your life feels shaky, like if your family members or friendships are going through trouble or health problems are scaring you or a loved one, remember that God is your rock-solid source of stability. He promises that you will not be shaken. Yes, things in your life might feel shaky sometimes—but no matter what happens, in the end God keeps you steady and strong and safe.

*Dear God, You are strong and steady all the time,
in every place I am and in every problem I might
have. When things around me feel shaky, please
remind me to lean on You, my solid Rock. Amen.*

GOD LOVES IN EXTRAORDINARY DETAIL

"Are not two small birds sold for a very small piece of money? And yet not one of the birds falls to the earth without your Father knowing it. God knows how many hairs you have on your head. So do not be afraid. You are more important than many small birds."
MATTHEW 10:29–31

No matter how close you are to your family and friends, there is no one who knows and loves you like God does. Your mom and dad might know a lot of details about you, and your friends might know all your favorite things, but none of them know how many hairs are on your head. That doesn't mean they don't love you—it just shows that God, who does know the exact number of hairs on your head, loves you more than anyone else ever could! And He gives you your family and friends as part of the way He shows you His extraordinary, detailed love. He cares about everything in His creation, even the tiniest of birds, but He knows and loves people most of all, and that definitely includes you!

Dear God, wow, I'm amazed how well You know me— even better than I know myself. Help me to focus on that truth and never forget it! Amen.

NOT AFRAID OF ANYTHING

*The Lord is my Shepherd. I will have everything I need.
He lets me rest in fields of green grass. He leads me beside
the quiet waters. He makes me strong again. He leads me in
the way of living right with Himself which brings honor to His
name. Yes, even if I walk through the valley of the shadow of
death, I will not be afraid of anything, because You are with
me. You have a walking stick with which to guide and one with
which to help. These comfort me. You are making a table of
food ready for me in front of those who hate me. You have
poured oil on my head. I have everything I need. For sure, You
will give me goodness and loving-kindness all the days of my
life. Then I will live with You in Your house forever.*
PSALM 23

The Lord God is your Shepherd, leading you and giving you
everything you need. Let this famous psalm encourage you
and make you brave. Memorize it and repeat it throughout
your day, in any situation you are facing!

*Dear God, because You lead me and care
for me, I have nothing to be afraid of.
Not a thing! Thank You, thank You! Amen.*

EXTRAORDINARY GRATITUDE

There was a woman in the city who was a sinner.
She knew Jesus was eating in the house of the proud
religious law-keeper. She brought a jar of special perfume.
Then she stood behind Him by His feet and cried. Her tears
wet His feet and she dried them with her hair. She kissed
His feet and put the special perfume on them.
LUKE 7:37–38

This woman in the Bible had such great love and gratitude for Jesus. She had done a lot of bad things in her life, but she trusted Jesus as her Savior to forgive them. And so she was very grateful for Him and wanted to show Jesus her thanks in an extraordinary way. The proud law-keepers there did not like that Jesus allowed this woman to act this way, but Jesus said, "I tell you, her many sins are forgiven because she loves much. But the one who has been forgiven little, loves little" (Luke 7:47).

🌼 🌼 🌼

Dear God, thank You for the example of the woman who
washed Jesus' feet with her tears and gave Him special
perfume. I want to show my love and gratitude for
my Savior in extraordinary ways too! Amen.

DARKNESS TURNED TO LIGHT

*"I will lead the blind by a way that they do not know. I will
lead them in paths they do not know. I will turn darkness into
light in front of them. And I will make the bad places smooth.
These are the things I will do and I will not leave them."*
Isaiah 42:16

Have you ever stubbed your toe in the dark because you were
stumbling around? Ouch! You might feel like that in your life
sometimes, like you just can't see the right way to go when
you have a big choice to make or when you're facing a big
problem. So trust this scripture where God promises to turn
darkness into light and make bad places smooth for His people. He will open up new paths for you when you don't know
what to do or where to go, and He will never leave you!

*Dear God, I'm following You even when I can't see where
You are taking me. I trust You to take me on good paths
and make all the rough spots smooth. Thank You for
leading me and never leaving me. Amen.*

CHOOSE EXTRAORDINARY JOY

*Be full of joy always because you belong to the Lord.
Again I say, be full of joy! Let all people see how
gentle you are. The Lord is coming again soon.*
PHILIPPIANS 4:4–5

Always be full of joy? Really? you might be asking. That's easier said than done sometimes. What's joyful about getting a cavity filled or your braces tightened? What's joyful about getting a test back and seeing a bad grade after you studied the best you could? What's joyful about a best friend moving away or a loved one dying? And it's true, those things are not joyful. But you can still be full of joy in the midst of them because of one important truth if you trust Jesus as your Savior—you belong to God! All those unjoyful things that happen here on earth are just temporary, but the perfect home God is creating for us in heaven lasts forever. Jesus is coming again soon, and we will live there forever with Him— with no cavities and no bad grades ever again!

*Dear God, remind me every moment that I belong
to You! That's where my steady, true joy comes from
no matter what is going on around me. Amen.*

WHEN YOU FEEL WALKED ALL OVER

All day long those who hate me have walked on me. For there are many who fight against me with pride. When I am afraid, I will trust in You. I praise the Word of God. I have put my trust in God. I will not be afraid. What can only a man do to me? All day long they change my words to say what I did not say. They are always thinking of ways to hurt me. They go after me as in a fight. They hide themselves. They watch my steps, as they have waited to take my life. Because they are bad, do not let them get away. Bring down the people in Your anger, O God.

PSALM 56:2–7

This psalm sounds like it's describing some pretty awful bullies, and maybe you can relate a little to kids acting mean or walking all over you. But even as all these awful things are happening, the writer is choosing to trust in God. He's remembering he does not need to be afraid of people when the one, true, all-powerful God is on his side.

❀ ❀ ❀

Dear God, when I feel bullied and walked all over, don't let me forget that You see and know what's going on, and You will protect and fight for me. Amen.

EXTRAORDINARY EXAMPLE

Let no one show little respect for you because you are young.
Show other Christians how to live by your life. They should be
able to follow you in the way you talk and in what you do.
Show them how to live in faith and in love and in holy living.
1 Timothy 4:12

Even when you're young, you can choose to show those
around you how to live the best kind of life. You can learn
God's Word and follow it. You can choose to love God and
others well and show respect and kindness. You can work
hard at everything you do as a way to bring praise to God,
not yourself. You won't do all this perfectly, and that's okay.
But you can try your very best and know that as a young person living your life devoted to God, you are setting a truly
extraordinary example for others to follow!

Dear God, please help me even while I'm so young to set
a great example of how to love and live for You! Amen.

REMEMBER ALL GOD IS ABLE TO DO!

"Let the name of God be honored forever and ever, for wisdom and power belong to Him. He changes the times and the years. He takes kings away, and puts kings in power. He gives wisdom to wise men and much learning to men of understanding. He makes known secret and hidden things. He knows what is in the darkness. Light is with Him. I give thanks and praise to You, O God of my fathers. For You have given me wisdom and power. Even now You have made known what we asked of You."
DANIEL 2:20–23

You've probably heard of the great faith and obedience and courage of Daniel, who was thrown into the lions' den in the Bible—and survived because of God's miracle of shutting the lions' mouths. This scripture in Daniel 2 is part of Daniel's prayer to God, worshipping Him for all the extraordinary things He is able to do. Let it inspire your prayers too!

Dear God, like Daniel, please help me to remember everything You are able to do as I pray. I want to worship You and have great courage because I focus on Your power and works— in the past, right now, and in the future too. Amen.

EXTRAORDINARY GOOD NEWS

I am not ashamed of the Good News. It is the power of God. It is the way He saves men from the punishment of their sins if they put their trust in Him. It is for the Jew first and for all other people also. The Good News tells us we are made right with God by faith in Him. Then, by faith we live that new life through Him. The Holy Writings say, "A man right with God lives by faith."

ROMANS 1:16–17

We all have things we feel embarrassed about or ashamed of, but we should never feel embarrassed or ashamed of Jesus. Like Paul in the Bible, we should all want to be able to say this—that we are not ashamed of the good news that Jesus came to earth to live a perfect life and teach us, then died on the cross to pay for our sins, and then rose to life again and offers us eternal life too. When we share this good news with others, we help spread God's power to save people from their sins.

Dear God, help me never to be ashamed to share the good news about Jesus! Thank You for wanting to save all people from their sins! Amen.

CHOOSE COMPASSION

Jesus said, "A man was going down from Jerusalem to the city of Jericho. Robbers came out after him. They took his clothes off and beat him. Then they went away, leaving him almost dead. . . . Then a man from the country of Samaria came by. He went up to the man. As he saw him, he had loving-pity on him. He got down and put oil and wine on the places where he was hurt and put cloth around them. Then the man from Samaria put this man on his own donkey. He took him to a place where people stay for the night and cared for him. The next day the man from Samaria was ready to leave. He gave the owner of that place two pieces of money to care for him. He said to him, 'Take care of this man. If you use more than this, I will give it to you when I come again.' "
Luke 10:30, 33–35

Two people just walked on by the poor man who had been robbed and beaten. But then a Samaritan man chose compassion and helped a stranger, going above and beyond to make sure he was well cared for. Jesus told this story to give us an example of loving our neighbors and showing that our neighbor is anyone in need.

❁ ❁ ❁

Dear God, I want to choose compassion for my neighbors in need. Show me the best ways to care for others. Amen.

KING AND FATHER FOREVER

*We give honor and thanks to the King Who lives forever.
He is the One Who never dies and Who is never seen.
He is the One Who knows all things. He is the only God.*
1 TIMOTHY 1:17

Of all the powerful kings and queens and royal people throughout history, only one King is the one true God who lives forever and knows everything. How awesome that He is not some far-off, too-good-for-you god. No, He loves you and wants to be close to you. He is your heavenly Father who sent His one and only Son to die for you so that you could be saved from your sin and have a relationship with Him as close as a child's relationship with the very best kind of daddy (see Romans 8:15–17).

Dear God, You are my one and only true King forever! Thank You that You love me dearly as Your own child and want to be close to me and bless me with good things. Amen.

EXTRAORDINARY LIKE TABITHA

*A woman who was a follower lived in the city of
Joppa. Her name was Tabitha, or Dorcas. She did
many good things and many acts of kindness.*
ACTS 9:36

Tabitha was known for being good and kind and making lovely clothing for others. Sadly, she became sick and died, but her friends knew of a special man named Peter. He was Jesus' disciple and was known to heal the sick and raise the dead back to life in Jesus' name. So two of Tabitha's friends went to Peter and begged him to come and help Tabitha. Peter agreed and went to the house where they had laid her body. Her friends were gathered around her, crying, and they showed Peter all the nice clothes she had made them. Then Peter told them all to leave the room, and he knelt down and prayed. Then he said to Tabitha, "Get up." And she opened her eyes and sat up! By the power of Jesus, Peter had raised Tabitha back to life! And probably she then went right back to doing the many good and kind things she loved to do.

*Dear God, Tabitha inspires me to be generous and to use
the talents You've given me to provide for and encourage
others. And it's so awesome how Peter was able to raise her
back to life because You are the God of miracles! Amen.*

PROVING YOUR FAITH

With this hope you can be happy even if you need to have
sorrow and all kinds of tests for awhile. These tests have
come to prove your faith and to show that it is good. Gold,
which can be destroyed, is tested by fire. Your faith is
worth much more than gold and it must be tested also.
1 PETER 1:6–7

When we keep our faith in Jesus as our Savior through all kinds of sadness and hard times in our lives, we prove our faith is real. Saying we love and trust Jesus during happy, good times is easy, but saying we love and trust Him even when we go through bad times is not so easy. Your faith is the most valuable thing about you, worth so much more than gold or any kind of treasure. So, every day, keep asking God to grow and strengthen it, and don't be surprised when it is tested sometimes. Hold on to God during those testing times and see how your faith develops an extraordinary shine when you never let it go.

Dear God, please help me not to be surprised by the sad
or hard times that test my faith. I want to keep holding on
to You and prove that my faith is real and true! Amen.

NO ONE SAVES LIKE GOD SAVES

Then the man who spread news for the king said in a loud voice, "This is what you must do, O people of every nation and language: When you hear the sound of the horns and harps, and all kinds of music, you are to get down on your knees and worship the object of gold that King Nebuchadnezzar has set up. Whoever does not get down and worship will be thrown at once into the big and hot fire."

DANIEL 3:4–6

Do you know this story of three friends and a fire in the Bible? The friends, named Shadrach, Meshach, and Abednego, loved God and refused to bow down to worship the false god the king had set up. So they were thrown into a blazing hot fire that should have killed them. Instead, they walked around in the fire and never burned even one hair. In fact, they even had some company—an angel of God! When the king let them out, he praised the one true God and decreed that no one could speak against Him. He said, "There is no other god able to save in this way" (Daniel 3:29).

Dear God, it's so true—no other god is able to save like You! I choose to honor You and never worship false gods. Amen.

EXTRAORDINARY SHEPHERD

"I am the Good Shepherd. The Good Shepherd gives His life for the sheep. One who is hired to watch the sheep is not the shepherd. He does not own the sheep. He sees the wolf coming and leaves the sheep. He runs away while the wolf gets the sheep and makes them run everywhere. The hired man runs away because he is hired. He does not care about the sheep. I am the Good Shepherd. I know My sheep and My sheep know Me."
JOHN 10:11–14

What do you think you'd look like as a sheep? Because you are one! Jesus taught about being the Good Shepherd, and then later He proved it by giving up His own life to save others from sin. Anyone who trusts in Jesus as Savior becomes a sheep under Jesus' care—and that's a wonderful creature to be.

Dear Jesus, thank You for letting me be Your sheep. I want to follow You forever! Amen.

KING FROM LONG AGO

God is still my King from long ago. He does saving works upon the earth. You divided the sea by Your power. You broke the heads of the large dragons in the waters. You crushed the heads of the Leviathan. And You fed him to the animals of the desert. It was You Who opened up the earth for water to flow out. And You dried up rivers that flow forever. The day is Yours. And the night is Yours. You have set the light and the sun in their places. You have divided all the lands and seas and nations of the earth. You have made summer and winter.
PSALM 74:12–17

Kings and dragons and sea monsters? This all sounds like something from a wild fiction book, but it's actually praise to God for the works He has done. When you choose to trust God, you are making a wise decision, because God has a ton of experience doing great and mighty things!

Dear God, You are so much more than my brain can imagine! I praise You for all You have done in the past and all You will do in the future. I'm so thankful to be Your child. Amen.

CHOOSE BETTER

*When someone does something bad to you, do not do the same
thing to him. When someone talks about you, do not talk about
him. Instead, pray that good will come to him. You were called
to do this so you might receive good things from God.*

1 PETER 3:9

You can learn such good lessons when someone is mean or
rude or does bad things to you. You can learn what *not* to do
to someone else. You can learn to choose better or "take the
high road." God calls us to take that higher road and not pay
them back. In fact, He wants us to pray that good things will
come to the people who do bad to us. That's sure not easy,
but remember that God wants to bless you when you obey
this calling. Ask Him to help you with this, and then see how
He rewards you!

❁ ❁ ❁

*Dear God, I pray for those who do bad things to me. Please help
them to stop doing bad things and instead know and want to
share Your love. Please bless them with good things to fill their
lives. Help me not to want to pay them back in some mean way
but instead to trust in You to take care of everything. Amen.*

EXTRAORDINARY LOVE

"For God so loved the world that He gave His only Son. Whoever puts his trust in God's Son will not be lost but will have life that lasts forever. For God did not send His Son into the world to say it is guilty. He sent His Son so the world might be saved from the punishment of sin by Him."
JOHN 3:16–17

Hopefully you've heard the scripture John 3:16–17 before. It's one of the most famous passages in all of the Bible, and it's one you should never forget. It sums up God's extraordinary love for you. He loves you and everyone in the world so incredibly much that He gave up His only Son, Jesus, to die on the cross to pay the price for the sin of every person. And then Jesus rose to life again, showing how He conquers death and gives forever life to anyone who believes in Him as Savior.

❀ ❀ ❀

Dear God, thank You for Your extraordinary love for me and for all people. Thank You for sending Jesus to die to save the world from the punishment of sin. Thank You that He rose to life again and that I have forever life too because I believe in Him as my one and only Savior. Amen.

ALPHA AND OMEGA

"I am the First and the Last.
I am the beginning and the end."
REVELATION 22:13

Jesus says several times in the Bible that He is the first and the last, the beginning and the end. Some Bible translations use the words *Alpha* and *Omega*, the names of the first and last letters in the Greek alphabet. To say that He is both of these letters is a way of saying that Jesus is everything and He has always existed. You could say in our alphabet that He is A and He is Z! He has gone before us, and He comes behind us. He is always around us. It's hard for our minds to understand this reality, but it's wonderful to trust that Jesus knows and has always known the whole story of our lives.

Dear Jesus, You are the beginning and end of all things.
I am so blessed to call You my Savior. Amen.

PRAISE AND PRAY ALL THE TIME

I will honor the Lord at all times. His praise will always be in my mouth. My soul will be proud to tell about the Lord. Let those who suffer hear it and be filled with joy. Give great honor to the Lord with me. Let us praise His name together.

PSALM 34:1–3

Do you ever get in trouble for giving some sass to your parents? Or saying mean things to a sibling? It can be hard to be careful with your words. But if praise to God is always in your mouth like this psalm says, then there won't be much room for any complaining or grumpy or mean talk, right? Another scripture says, "You must pray at all times as the Holy Spirit leads you to pray. Pray for the things that are needed. You must watch and keep on praying. Remember to pray for all Christians" (Ephesians 6:18). Do your best to remember these two scriptures so your mind and tongue will always be busy doing good things instead of maybe getting you into trouble!

✿ ✿ ✿

Dear God, I want to choose praise and prayer more often and keep them in my mind and mouth. Please help me! Amen.

LIKE GRASSHOPPERS

It is God Who sits on the throne above the earth.
The people living on the earth are like grasshoppers.
He spreads out the heavens like a curtain. He spreads them
out like a tent to live in. It is He Who brings rulers down to
nothing. He makes the judges of the earth as nothing. . . .
Lift up your eyes and see. Who has made these stars? It is
the One Who leads them out by number. He calls them all
by name. Because of the greatness of His strength, and
because He is strong in power, not one of them is missing.
ISAIAH 40:22–23, 26

You're just like a grasshopper to God! But that doesn't mean you don't matter to Him! This passage is just describing more of God's awesome greatness. He is so big and mighty that we are all like little bugs to Him. He spread out the skies as easily as if they were curtains. He has the power to defeat any ruler or king. He made the stars and counts them and even has a name for every single one. And this same amazing God knows and cares about every single detail of you too!

Dear God, I'm so thankful that I matter to
such an extraordinary God as You! You fill me
with such love and courage because I know
You are always taking care of me. Amen.

EXTRAORDINARY LIKE MARTHA AND MARY

*Martha had a sister named Mary. Mary sat
at the feet of Jesus and listened to all He said.*
LUKE 10:39

Two sisters named Mary and Martha were excited to welcome Jesus into their home. Martha was very good at hosting and knew all the details of planning and preparing for visitors. Since Jesus was such an extraspecial guest, she wanted everything to be perfect for Him so He could have a nice place to rest and relax and eat a delicious meal. But Martha grew very frustrated with Mary because when Jesus arrived, Mary didn't help her with all the work of hosting. She simply sat at Jesus' feet to listen to everything He had to say. Both sisters loved Jesus and were showing it in their own ways. But Jesus lovingly told Martha that Mary had chosen what was best, not fussing much over the details of hosting Him but simply enjoying His company and listening to His teaching.

*Dear Jesus, I want to show my love to You in
extraspecial details, like Martha, but I always want
to choose the best way by enjoying simply being
with You, like Mary. You are truly extraordinary, Jesus,
and I want to listen to every word You say. Amen.*

EXTRAORDINARY CREATION

*So the heavens and the earth were completed, and
all that is in them. On the seventh day God ended
His work which He had done. And He rested on the
seventh day from all His work which He had done.*
GENESIS 2:1–2

When you look at a beautiful sunset, when you go for a hike in
a thick forest, when you swim in a rippling lake, when you pick
a pretty wildflower. . .when you do anything that makes you
focus on and appreciate the natural world around you, spend
some time praising our Creator God! The natural world He
has designed and given us is truly extraordinary and reminds
us in countless ways how awesome He is. He planned and created land and air and sea, plants and animals and you and me,
with incredible love and detail and purpose.

*Dear God, thank You for Your awesome
creation. It reminds me every day how
incredible You are, and I praise You! Amen.*

THE BEST BOSS

If your sinful old self is the boss over your mind, it leads to death. But if the Holy Spirit is the boss over your mind, it leads to life and peace. The mind that thinks only of ways to please the sinful old self is fighting against God. It is not able to obey God's Laws. It never can. Those who do what their sinful old selves want to do cannot please God. But you are not doing what your sinful old selves want you to do. You are doing what the Holy Spirit tells you to do, if you have God's Spirit living in you.

ROMANS 8:6–9

Before we trust in Jesus as Savior, the sinfulness in us tells us what to do. If we let sin be our boss, we will choose self-ishness and greed and only look out for ourselves. But once we trust Jesus, we have His Holy Spirit living inside us. The Holy Spirit is the best boss who always wants the very best for us—a life of loving God and loving others and being filled with joy from sharing the good news and spreading hope for eternal life.

❀ ❀ ❀

Dear God, thank You for saving me and giving me the very best boss—Your Holy Spirit. Help me to choose to obey every day! Amen.

EVEN IF

Even if an army gathers against me, my heart will not be afraid.
Even if war rises against me, I will be sure of You.
PSALM 27:3

Let this scripture inspire you to think of all kinds of "even if" statements to proclaim the extraordinary courage God gives you, like this.

"Even if this big, loud storm doesn't stop, I will not be afraid because I trust You to take care of me and my family, God!"

"Even if this test tomorrow is so hard, I will trust You to help me do my best, God!"

"Even if this sickness does not go away, I know You love and care for me in the middle of it, God!"

"Even if you don't heal this injury here on earth like I know You can, I trust that You heal forever in heaven, God!"

"Even if I make mistakes, I know You love and forgive me, God!"

❁ ❁ ❁

Dear God, thank You that my heart doesn't
need to be afraid of anything and that I
can be totally sure of You! Amen.

FOREVER AT HOME

"Do not let your heart be troubled. You have put your trust in God, put your trust in Me also. There are many rooms in My Father's house. If it were not so, I would have told you. I am going away to make a place for you. After I go and make a place for you, I will come back and take you with Me. Then you may be where I am. You know where I am going and you know how to get there."

John 14:1–4

We have an extraordinary home waiting for us in heaven—in God's house! Jesus talked about its many rooms. Do you ever dream about what those rooms might be like? They will be far cooler than anything we can imagine! Talk to God and tell Him what you hope heaven will be like, and then tell Him you simply trust it will be the very best because we will live with Him there.

Dear God, I believe that heaven will be awesome! I'm so thankful Jesus has saved me from my sin so that I get to spend forever at home with You! Amen.

AN EXTRAORDINARY MAP

*Thomas said to Jesus, "Lord, we do not know where
You are going. How can we know the way to get there?"
Jesus said, "I am the Way and the Truth and the Life.
No one can go to the Father except by Me."*
JOHN 14:5–6

Jesus' follower Thomas wanted details, maybe even a map,
to know exactly how to get to the home Jesus promised He
was getting ready. But Jesus said He is the Way, Truth, and
Life, and no one goes to God except through Him. In other
words, Jesus *is* the map to follow to heaven. We follow Him by
reading His Word and doing our best to live like Him, always
trusting that He alone saved us from sin when He died on the
cross. And because He rose to life again, we know we will too!

*Dear Jesus, thank You for being our map to heaven! I trust
You are the one and only Way, Truth, and Life! Amen.*

GIVE GOD ALL THE CREDIT

*If anyone wants to be proud, he should be proud of what
the Lord has done. It is not what a man thinks and says of
himself that is important. It is what God thinks of him.*
2 CORINTHIANS 10:17–18

Of course you feel happy when you accomplish something
cool, right? And that's great! Just don't forget to always give
God credit for each good and cool thing you do. He deserves
every bit of praise and worship because He is the One who
gives you your gifts and abilities.

❀ ❀ ❀

*Dear God, please help me to use the cool talents and abilities
You've given me to share Your love with others. And when I
do make mistakes, please forgive me and help me to do better
next time. Please remind me that it doesn't matter what others
think about me; it only matters what You think of me! Amen.*

AN EXTRAORDINARY CATCH

*When He had finished speaking, He said to Simon, "Push
out into the deep water. Let down your nets for some fish."
Simon said to Him, "Teacher, we have worked all night and we
have caught nothing. But because You told me to, I will let the
net down." When they had done this, they caught so many fish,
their net started to break. They called to their friends working
in the other boat to come and help them. They came and
both boats were so full of fish they began to sink.*

Luke 5:4–7

Jesus helped the fishermen catch far more than they could
have imagined. They had just spent the whole night fishing
and had caught nothing, but Jesus only had to say the words,
and suddenly the fish were everywhere—enough to break
their nets and sink their boat! Never forget that God is able
to provide so much more than you expect. Keep trusting Him
and asking Him for everything you need.

*Dear God, You go above and beyond to show how You love
to help and provide. I know You can for me too! Amen.*

NO FAKES

Our God is in the heavens. He does whatever He wants to do. Their gods are silver and gold, the work of human hands. They have mouths but they cannot speak. They have eyes but they cannot see. They have ears but they cannot hear. They have noses but they cannot smell. They have hands but they cannot feel. They have feet but they cannot walk. They cannot make a sound come out of their mouths. Those who make them and trust them will be like them.

PSALM 115:3–8

This scripture compares our one true God with the fake gods of the world that some people make for themselves. It describes how silly those fake gods are, with useless mouths, eyes, ears, noses, hands, and feet. But people often make fake gods because they don't really want to serve or worship anyone but themselves. And so they will end up as useless and meaningless as those fake gods. But to trust and worship and obey our extraordinary God is to live the life you were created for, with love and hope and peace forever.

❀ ❀ ❀

Dear God, I'm so thankful I trust in You and not a fake god. Help me to keep living for You and sharing You with others. Amen.

THE ONE WHO LIFTS YOUR HEAD

You, O Lord, are a covering around me, my shining-greatness, and the One Who lifts my head. I was crying to the Lord with my voice. And He answered me from His holy mountain. I lay down and slept, and I woke up again, for the Lord keeps me safe.
PSALM 3:3–5

Sometimes life feels so sad or frustrating or scary that you just need to go to your bedroom and cry your eyes out. And that's okay! As you do, think of God like your favorite blanket comforting you, like this scripture says He is the covering around you. He is the One who helps you and gives you "shining-greatness" again. He lifts your head and wants to help you get out of bed and face the hard things going on. Remember that it's good to cry out to God and let out all your feelings, but then always let Him lift your head again!

Dear God, I'm so grateful You comfort and cover me when I'm crying to You. And then You lift my head again. I can face anything with You as my constant help. Amen.

EXTRAORDINARY LIKE LOIS AND EUNICE

*I remember your true faith. It is the same faith your
grandmother Lois had and your mother Eunice had.
I am sure you have that same faith also.*

2 TIMOTHY 1:5

The Bible doesn't talk a lot about two women named Lois
and Eunice, but what it does say can inspire us. These two
women were the grandmother and mother to a man named
Timothy who was a young Christian. His friend was Paul,
who wrote many of the letters in the New Testament of the
Bible. The book of 2 Timothy is one of Paul's letters to Timothy to encourage him in his faith. Paul reminds Timothy of
the true faith of his grandma and mom, Lois and Eunice. What
an honor for these ladies to be remembered like this! As you
grow up, think about how you want your faith to be remembered. Be strong and keep growing in it so that others will say
your faith was always true.

*Dear God, I want to be known for having
true faith in You that I share with others,
just like Lois and Eunice. Amen.*

GOD OF ALL WEATHER

"God thunders with His great voice. He does great things which we cannot understand. For He says to the snow, 'Fall on the earth,' and to the rain, 'Be strong.' He stops the work of every man, that all men may know His work. Then the wild animals go to their holes, and stay where they live. The storm comes from the south, and the cold from the north. Water becomes ice by the breath of God. The wide waters become ice. He loads the heavy clouds with water and they send out His lightning. It changes its path and turns around by His leading, doing whatever He tells it to do on the earth where people live. He causes it to happen for punishment, or for His world, or because of His love."
JOB 37:5–13

Scientists today can make all kinds of good predictions about the weather, but no one can control it except the One who created it—our extraordinary God! Thank Him for all the ways weather helps our world, like the way sunshine and rain help to grow our food. And even when the weather doesn't go the way you want, like when lightning cancels your softball game, trust God and choose to praise Him as the powerful One who commands it, knowing He uses it to work out His good plans.

🌸 🌸 🌸

Dear God, You are awesome and mighty in Your control of the weather. I praise You and thank You for it all! Amen.

NOTHING CAN KEEP HIS LOVE AWAY

Nothing can keep us from the love of God. Death cannot!
Life cannot! Angels cannot! Leaders cannot! Any other
power cannot! Hard things now or in the future cannot!
The world above or the world below cannot! Any other
living thing cannot keep us away from the love of God
which is ours through Christ Jesus our Lord.
ROMANS 8:38–39

God's extraordinary love is totally unstoppable in your life.
This is such a powerful scripture to remind you that you
don't have to be afraid of anything! No matter what you go
through, God is with you, and He is loving you and helping
you in the midst of it. Nothing and no one can ever stop or
defeat Him. Think of times when you felt completely helpless
and hopeless, but then love and help came through anyway.
That was God at work! Remember those times and trust Him
for more of them in the future.

Dear God, I'm so grateful for reminders that nothing
keeps Your love away from me. Thank You for all the
ways You've loved and helped me so far in my life and
all the ways I know You will in the future. Amen.

EXTRAORDINARY EQUALITY

You are now children of God because you have put your trust in Christ Jesus. All of you who have been baptized to show you belong to Christ have become like Christ. God does not see you as a Jew or as a Greek. He does not see you as a servant or as a person free to work. He does not see you as a man or as a woman. You are all one in Christ.
GALATIANS 3:26–28

You might hear the word *equality* a lot these days, but it's important to remember that only Jesus gives true equality. Because of sin in the world, people will never get equality exactly right. There will always be bad people trying to say some groups of people are better than others. But don't ever listen to or join them. In God's eyes, because of Jesus, every single person is the same in value. We all matter so much to God that He sent Jesus to die to save us from our sins. And when anyone trusts in Jesus, they become a child of the one true God, the King of all kings. That makes all God's children equally royal!

✿ ✿ ✿

Dear God, thank You that anyone can be Your child by trusting that only Jesus saves. You offer the only true equality through Him. Help me to share this awesome truth with others in this sinful world. Amen.

EXTRAORDINARY LIKE MARY MAGDALENE

It was the first day of the week. Mary Magdalene came to the grave early in the morning while it was still dark. She saw that the stone had been pushed away from the grave. She ran to Simon Peter and the other follower whom Jesus loved. She said to them, "They have taken the Lord out of the grave. We do not know where they have put Him."

JOHN 20:1–2

There are several women named Mary in the Bible. Mary Magdalene was a woman who'd had a terrible life before she met Jesus. He cast seven demons out of her, and she was so grateful that she became a close follower of Jesus. When Jesus was crucified, she was there, and she must have felt incredibly sad and scared. But she was also there when Jesus rose from the dead, and then she must have been completely overwhelmed with joy! The Bible tells us she was the very first to see Jesus again after He had come back to life. That's an extraordinary blessing for sure!

Dear God, help me to remember that You rescue people from terrible situations and then You bless them incredibly, just as You rescued and blessed Mary Magdalene. Amen.

TOTAL TRUTH

This is what the Lord Who made the heavens, the God
Who planned and made the earth, and everything in it
and did not make it a waste place, but made it a place
for people to live in, says, "I am the Lord, and there is
no other. I have not spoken in secret in some dark land.
I did not say to the children of Jacob, 'Look for Me for
nothing.' I the Lord speak the truth. I say what is right."
ISAIAH 45:18–19

Telling the truth is so important, especially when it seems like
fewer and fewer people care about it these days. No matter
who is spreading lies all around you, though, there is always
one source of total truth—God. And He tells us His total truth
in His Word, the Bible. We need to keep coming back to it
again and again, reading and studying as much as we can, to
know how to live right in the world God has made.

Dear God, remind me that You and Your Word are
absolute, total truth. Please help me to know Your
truth and grow in it more and more—and to always
tell the truth and share truth with others. Amen.

EXTRAORDINARY GRACE

*He said to Jesus, "Lord, remember me when You come
into Your holy nation." Jesus said to him, "For sure,
I tell you, today you will be with Me in Paradise."*
LUKE 23:42–43

When Jesus was dying on the cross, one of the criminals next
to Him believed in Him and asked Jesus to remember him.
And Jesus promised that the criminal would be in paradise
that very day when he died. This account shows how full of
grace our extraordinary Savior is. He gives grace until even
the very last moments of life, wanting everyone to believe in
Him and accept Him as Savior. If you have friends and loved
ones who do not trust in Jesus, keep on praying for them
and sharing His love. God wants to give them every chance
possible.

❀ ❀ ❀

*Dear Jesus, thank You for the example of the criminal
beside You who believed at the last moment. That gives
me so much hope for people I know who don't yet trust
in You. I will keep on sharing Your truth and love with
them. Please turn their hearts to You! Amen.*

EXTRAORDINARY RESPECT:
PART 1

*Children, as Christians, obey your parents. This is the right
thing to do. Respect your father and mother. This is the
first Law given that had a promise. The promise is this:
If you respect your father and mother, you will live a
long time and your life will be full of many good things.*
EPHESIANS 6:1–3

If you choose to happily obey your parents out of love and
respect for them, you will set yourself apart as truly extraordinary among kids today. And God's Word promises you will
be rewarded. God wants you to obey Him, and He wants you
to obey Mom and Dad. You honor Him when you honor them.

*Dear God, please forgive me when I mess up and
dishonor or disobey my parents. Please help me to
quickly make it right with them and then do better
at lovingly respecting and obeying them. Amen.*

EXTRAORDINARY RESPECT: PART 2

Do not speak sharp words to an older man.
Talk with him as if he were a father. . . .
Talk to older women as mothers.
1 TIMOTHY 5:1–2

We all should also show great respect to those who are older than us, and that includes our leaders and teachers. Hebrews 13:17 says, "Obey your leaders and do what they say. They keep watch over your souls. They have to tell God what they have done. They should have joy in this and not be sad. If they are sad, it is no help to you." To be wise, not only should we be showing respect to our elders and leaders, but we should always be talking to and learning from them as well.

Dear God, help me to have great respect for my leaders and my elders. Please give me good opportunities to talk to and learn from them so that I can gain some of their wisdom. Amen.

OVERPOWERING HOPE

*We want you to know for sure about those who have
died. You have no reason to have sorrow as those who
have no hope. We believe that Jesus died and then came
to life again. Because we believe this, we know that God
will bring to life again all those who belong to Jesus.*

1 THESSALONIANS 4:13–14

Maybe you've experienced the loss of a family member or
friend. The pain and sadness can be awful. But even while you
cry and miss them, you can have hope that overpowers the
pain and sadness, because if your loved one trusted Jesus,
then they will be brought to life again just like Jesus rose
again. That is an extraordinary comfort—and it should motivate us to share the good news of Jesus with those around
us. Just like God does, we should want all people to be saved
from sin (see 1 Timothy 2:4).

*Dear God, I'm so very grateful for the hope You give us
because of Jesus. Help me to share the good news and
help others put their trust in You so we all can be raised
to life again and live with You forever. Amen.*

COPY THE KING

"The Son of Man came not to be cared for. He came to care for others. He came to give His life so that many could be bought by His blood and made free from the punishment of sin."
MATTHEW 20:28

Another name for Jesus is the Son of Man. He is King of all kings and Lord of all lords, but He sure didn't come in the way we normally think of royalty—important people who have servants and staff waiting on them hand and foot. No, Jesus came to serve and care for us. That reversal is truly extraordinary! He served and cared so much that He even gave His life for us to save us from sin. And once we trust Him as Savior, He asks us to copy Him in His love to serve and care for others so that they will want to know Him as Savior too.

✿ ✿ ✿

Dear Jesus, thank You for giving so much more than You ever want to get. You are the very best example of love and service. You are the most extraordinary and loving King, and I want to be as much like You as I can! Amen.

THROUGH THE THINGS HE HAS MADE

Men know about God. He has made it plain to them.
Men cannot say they do not know about God. From the
beginning of the world, men could see what God is like
through the things He has made. This shows His power
that lasts forever. It shows that He is God.
ROMANS 1:19–20

God has shown Himself through everything He has made in creation, so no person can say they know nothing about God. He can be seen in the tiny details of a pretty flower and in the highest peaks of a rocky mountain range. He can be seen in the extraordinary way our human bodies are designed and in the way animals know how to hunt for their food or build themselves a home. Our Creator God is awesome and worthy of all our praise!

Dear God, I love looking at Your work in all the things
You have made. Thank You for making Yourself known.
I pray that more people will want to grow closer to You
through Jesus because of seeing You in creation. Amen.

EXTRAORDINARY CHARACTER

A good name is to be chosen instead of many riches.
Favor is better than silver and gold. The rich and the poor
meet together. The Lord is the maker of them all. A wise
man sees sin and hides himself, but the foolish go on,
and are punished for it. The reward for not having pride
and having the fear of the Lord is riches, honor and life.
PROVERBS 22:1–4

A good name means a good reputation and good character.
When people hear your name, do you want them to think
of you in good ways or bad ways? Do you want to be known
for things like laziness or lying or rudeness or getting into
trouble? Or do you want to be known for things like doing
your best and being honest, fair, kind, and worthy of respect?
Choose now while you are young to do your best to have extraordinary character. Live for God and obey His ways of love
and fairness and honesty.

Dear God, I want to be known for good character qualities.
Please help me to honor You by having a good name. Amen.

ALL THINGS NEW

Then I saw a new heaven and a new earth. . . . I heard a loud voice coming from heaven. It said, "See! God's home is with men. He will live with them. They will be His people. God Himself will be with them. He will be their God. God will take away all their tears. There will be no more death or sorrow or crying or pain. All the old things have passed away." Then the One sitting on the throne said, "See! I am making all things new."
REVELATION 21:1, 3–5

The Bible doesn't give us a whole lot of detail about what forever life will be like, probably because our minds could never fully understand how awesome it will be (see 1 Corinthians 2:9). But it does tell us everything will be new and there will be no more death or sorrow or crying or pain. That fact alone shows us how truly extraordinary it will be!

Dear God, I can't even imagine how amazing it will be when You make Your home with us in the new heaven and earth You have planned. Until then, please keep me close to You, through Your Word and through prayer, as I do the good things You have for me in this life. Thank You! Amen.

EXTRAORDINARY FAITH HEROES

Because Sarah had faith, she was able to have a child long after she was past the age to have children. She had faith to believe that God would do what He promised. Abraham was too old to have children. But from this one man came a family with as many in it as the stars in the sky and as many as the sand by the sea.
HEBREWS 11:11–12

Do you have faith to believe that God will do what He has promised? Anytime you feel like your faith is weak, Hebrews 11 is a great chapter to read to strengthen it again. It will remind you of many Bible heroes—including extraordinary Sarah who trusted God would let her have a baby even though she was over ninety years old—who continued to believe that God would do what He promised even when it seemed impossible! Whatever you are needing God to do that might seem totally impossible, keep trusting Him today and every day!

Dear God, I want to be like Sarah and the many heroes in the Bible who had superstrong faith in You! Amen.

ONE TRUE RELIGION

We need such a Religious Leader Who made the way for man to go to God. Jesus is holy and has no guilt. He has never sinned and is different from sinful men. He has the place of honor above the heavens. Christ is not like other religious leaders. They had to give gifts every day on the altar in worship for their own sins first and then for the sins of the people. Christ did not have to do that. He gave one gift on the altar and that gift was Himself. It was done once and it was for all time.
HEBREWS 7:26–27

You might hear people say that all religions are the same, but it's just not true. Belief in Jesus as God and as our one and only Savior is what's true. Jesus alone was (and is) perfect and holy and without sin. He gave His own life once and for all, for people of all time, and no other religion offers that kind of gift and love and miracle! To know Jesus as Savior is simply to believe in Him and accept His awesome gift of grace and eternal life, which He provided when He took away our sins by dying on the cross for them and then rising to life again.

Dear Jesus, thank You for giving Your life to save everyone who believes in You! There is no one else like You! You are God and You are the one true Savior, and I am so grateful for You! Amen.

EXTRAORDINARY RETURN

*We are to be looking for the great hope and the coming
of our great God and the One Who saves, Christ Jesus.
He gave Himself for us. He did this by buying us with His
blood and making us free from all sin. He gave Himself
so His people could be clean and want to do good.*
TITUS 2:13–14

Always be watching for Jesus to return. He promises He will,
and His return will be truly extraordinary! It might sound a
little scary sometimes because it will be unlike anything any
person has ever experienced, but it will be wonderful for everyone who loves and trusts Him. Mark 13:24–27 says: "After
those days of much trouble and pain and sorrow are over, the
sun will get dark. The moon will not give light. The stars will
fall from the sky. The powers in the heavens will be shaken.
Then they will see the Son of Man coming in the clouds with
great power and shining-greatness. He will send His angels.
They will gather together God's people from the four winds.
They will come from one end of the earth to the other end
of heaven."

❀ ❀ ❀

*Dear Jesus, I'm watching and waiting for You
to return and gather Your people, including me!
I love You and trust You! Amen.*

SCRIPTURE INDEX

OLD TESTAMENT

MORE BOOKS FOR COURAGEOUS GIRLS!

Dare to Be a Courageous Girl

This delightfully unique journal will challenge courageous girls to live boldly for God! With each turn of the page, girls will encounter a new "dare" from the easy-to-understand New Life Version of scripture alongside a brief devotional reading and thought-provoking journal prompt or "challenge" that encourages them to take action and obey God's Word.

Paperback / 978-1-64352-642-3 / $14.99

The Bible for Courageous Girls

Part of the exciting Courageous Girls series, this Bible provides complete Old and New Testament text in the easy-reading New Life™ Version, plus insert pages featuring full-color illustrations of bold, brave women such as Abigail, Deborah, Esther, Mary Magdalene, and Mary, mother of Jesus.

DiCarta / 978-1-64352-069-8 / $24.99

With your parent's permission, check out CourageousGirls.com where you'll discover additional positive, faith-building activities and resources!

BARBOUR
kidz
A Division of Barbour Publishing